ESP32 Arduino Programming Essentials: An Absolute Beginner Guide for IoT Development

First Edition
Sarful Hassan

Preface

Who This Book Is For

This book is designed for absolute beginners who are interested in learning to program the ESP32 microcontroller using the Arduino environment. Whether you are a student, a hobbyist, or a professional looking to explore the world of IoT (Internet of Things), this guide will take you step-by-step from the basics of setting up your development environment to creating your own projects.

No prior experience with programming or microcontrollers is required—all concepts are explained from the ground up with detailed examples. By the end of this book, you will have a solid foundation for building IoT projects using the ESP32.

How This Book Is Organized

The book is organized into a series of chapters that guide you through different topics, building up your understanding gradually:

- Chapter 1: Introduction to ESP32 — Learn about the ESP32 and ESP8266, their history, evolution, and pinout.
- Chapter 2: Variables and Data Types — Understand how to use variables and different data types to store information.
- Chapter 3: Control Structures — Master conditional statements, loops, and other control structures for programming logic.
- Chapter 4: Operators — Get familiar with arithmetic, comparison, and logical operators.
- Chapter 5: GPIO I/O Operations — Learn how to interact with hardware using the General Purpose Input/Output (GPIO) pins.
- Chapter 6: Timing and Delays — Discover how to use delay functions and non-blocking timing for efficient code execution.
- Chapter 7: Maths Functions — Utilize basic math functions, value mapping, and random number generation.

- Chapter 8: Data Type Conversions — Explore ways to convert between data types for flexibility in coding.
- Chapter 9: ESP32 Networking (Wi-Fi) — Connect the ESP32 to a Wi-Fi network and explore networking features.
- Chapter 10: Web Server — Learn to set up a web server with ESP32 to interact with devices over the internet.
- Chapter 11: ESP Deep Sleep Mode — Use deep sleep features for power-efficient projects.

Each chapter contains examples and practical projects to reinforce what you've learned, giving you hands-on experience.

What Was Left Out

To keep this book accessible and easy to understand, advanced topics like complex networking configurations, in-depth exploration of the ESP-IDF (Espressif IoT Development Framework), and specific low-level hardware optimizations have been left out. If you're interested in more advanced topics, we encourage you to continue your journey with additional resources.

Platform Release Notes

This book is based on the latest stable version of the ESP32 and Arduino development environment at the time of writing. As technology evolves rapidly, you may find updates available. Please check mechatronicslab.net for the most recent updates, errata, and additional resources.

Notes on the First Edition

This is the first edition of this book, aimed at providing a beginner-friendly guide to ESP32 and Arduino. We have strived to ensure that all information is accurate and easy to follow. If you encounter any issues, please feel free to contact us.

Conventions Used in This Book

- Code snippets are presented in a monospaced font for easy identification.
- Important notes are highlighted in boxes like this to draw your attention to key concepts or details.

- Projects are introduced with step-by-step instructions to ensure you can follow along easily.

Using Code Examples

You are free to use the code examples in this book for your own projects. We believe that learning to code should be hands-on, so feel free to experiment and modify the examples to suit your needs. You can find additional resources and code snippets at our online learning platform: mechatronicslab.net.

mechatronicslab.net Online Learning

We offer free online resources to complement your learning experience. Visit mechatronicslab.net for additional tutorials, sample projects, and support materials. If you have any questions, feel free to email us at mechatronicslab.net@gmail.com.

How to Contact Us

- Website: mechatronicslab.net
- Email: mechatronicslab.net@gmail.com

Copyright

All contents of this book are copyrighted by mechatronicslab.net. You are encouraged to use and share the information for personal learning purposes. Any commercial use requires prior permission from the author.

Disclaimer

The information in this book is provided for educational purposes only. While we have made every effort to ensure accuracy, mechatronicslab.net and the author take no responsibility for errors, omissions, or damages resulting from the use of the information provided.

Table of Contents

Chapter-1 Introduction to ESP32

1.Overview of ESP32 and ESP8266

The **ESP32** and **ESP8266** are microcontrollers developed by
Espressif Systems, commonly used in **Internet of Things (IoT)**
projects. These microcontrollers are known for their **built-in Wi-Fi**
capabilities, which make them highly popular for connecting devices
to the internet and creating smart, connected systems. Both are
affordable and widely used, but they have different levels of power,
features, and applications, making them suitable for different use
cases.

- **ESP32**: Designed to be a high-performance microcontroller with dual-core processing, Wi-Fi, and Bluetooth capabilities, the ESP32 is ideal for more advanced IoT projects. It is suitable for applications where more computing power, additional features, and enhanced connectivity are needed.
- **ESP8266**: Known for its low cost and built-in Wi-Fi, the ESP8266 is ideal for simpler IoT projects, particularly for beginners or budget-conscious makers. It's capable of handling basic tasks and is perfect for projects that do not require the higher performance or additional connectivity options found in the ESP32.

Introduction to ESP32

The **ESP32** is a powerful and versatile microcontroller unit (MCU) created by Espressif Systems, specifically designed to enable connected, smart, and interactive devices. The key highlights of the ESP32 are:

- **Dual-Core Processor**: The ESP32 features two Xtensa LX6 processors, each capable of running up to **240 MHz**. This dual-core setup makes it powerful enough for multitasking and managing different operations simultaneously, which is beneficial in many IoT scenarios.
- **Connectivity**: It supports **Wi-Fi** (802.11 b/g/n) and **Bluetooth**, including **Bluetooth Low Energy (BLE)**. This makes the ESP32 versatile, as it can connect to the internet or other devices via Bluetooth.
- **Power Management**: The ESP32 is known for its various **low-power modes**, which makes it ideal for battery-powered applications. It can operate in **deep sleep mode** with very low power consumption, which is an essential feature for IoT projects that need to last long on a single battery charge.
- **Peripherals and GPIO**: The ESP32 comes with a wide range of **GPIO (General Purpose Input/Output) pins**, which can be used to connect sensors, LEDs, buttons, and other devices. It also has built-in modules like **analog-to-**

digital converters (ADC), **touch sensors**, and a
temperature sensor.
- **Applications**: It is well-suited for **smart home automation**,
  wearables, **wireless sensors**, and **other advanced IoT**
  projects that require a high level of connectivity and
  computation power.

Introduction to ESP8266

The **ESP8266** is an earlier microcontroller model from Espressif
Systems, widely popular for its affordability and integrated Wi-Fi.
Key characteristics of the ESP8266 are:

- **Single-Core Processor**: The ESP8266 features a **32-bit**
  Tensilica L106 processor, running at speeds between **80**
  MHz and 160 MHz. While it's not as powerful as the ESP32,
  it is sufficient for less demanding IoT projects, especially
  those that don't require extensive data processing.
- **Built-in Wi-Fi**: The ESP8266 has a built-in **Wi-Fi module**,
  making it perfect for connecting small devices to the internet
  without needing an external Wi-Fi chip. It supports standard
  Wi-Fi protocols for internet access.
- **Cost-Effectiveness**: The ESP8266 is known for being
  highly affordable, which is why it became popular with
  hobbyists and makers. It provides a low-cost way to add Wi-
  Fi capabilities to electronics.
- **GPIO and Connectivity**: It has a limited number of **GPIO**
  pins compared to the ESP32, which limits the number of
  sensors and peripherals that can be connected
  simultaneously. Nevertheless, it supports common
  communication protocols like **SPI**, **I2C**, and **UART**, making it
  versatile enough for many smaller projects.
- **Applications**: The ESP8266 is ideal for simple projects such
  as **smart light switches**, **basic wireless sensors**, and
  simple automation devices where a low-cost solution is
  needed.

Comparison between ESP32 and ESP8266

To help understand the differences and choose between ESP32 and ESP8266, let's compare their features:

1. **Processing Power**:
   - ○ **ESP32**: Features a **dual-core processor**, running up to **240 MHz**, providing more processing power for demanding applications.
   - ○ **ESP8266**: Has a **single-core processor** running at **80-160 MHz**, sufficient for simple tasks and straightforward IoT projects.
2. **Connectivity**:
   - ○ **ESP32**: Offers both **Wi-Fi** and **Bluetooth (including BLE)** connectivity. This dual connectivity makes it ideal for projects that require a variety of communication options.
   - ○ **ESP8266**: Offers only **Wi-Fi** connectivity, making it great for basic IoT projects that involve internet communication without the need for Bluetooth.
3. **Power Consumption**:
   - ○ **ESP32**: Comes with advanced power-saving features, including multiple power modes (like **deep sleep mode**), which make it suitable for battery-operated projects.
   - ○ **ESP8266**: Also supports power-saving, but it is less efficient than the ESP32, which may affect long-term battery life in some projects.
4. **GPIO and Peripherals**:
   - ○ **ESP32**: Has more **GPIO pins** and a richer set of built-in peripherals, including touch sensors, analog inputs, and a temperature sensor, giving more flexibility for complex projects.
   - ○ **ESP8266**: Has fewer GPIO pins, limiting the number of devices that can be connected, but is still capable of handling basic hardware interfaces and common sensors.
5. **Price**:

- ○ **ESP8266**: **Cheaper** compared to the ESP32, making it the preferred option for budget projects and for beginners just getting into IoT.
- ○ **ESP32**: Slightly **more expensive** but worth the cost for projects that require more features and better performance.

6. **Suitability for Projects**:
    - ○ **ESP32**: Best for **advanced IoT projects**, requiring high processing power, Bluetooth connectivity, and multiple sensor inputs. Examples include **smart home automation systems**, **wearable devices**, and **complex sensors**.
    - ○ **ESP8266**: Great for **entry-level and basic IoT projects**, where cost and simplicity are the main factors. It is perfect for **home automation**, such as smart lights and switches, where only Wi-Fi is required.

History and Evolution of ESP8266 and ESP32

Release Timeline

The ESP8266 and ESP32 microcontrollers have significantly impacted the development of IoT solutions by providing affordable and powerful connectivity options. Here's a look at their release history:

- **ESP8266 Release Timeline**:
    - ○ **2014**: The **ESP8266** was first introduced by Espressif Systems, becoming a game changer due to its integrated Wi-Fi capabilities at a very low cost. It initially gained popularity with hobbyists and DIY makers.
    - ○ **Late 2014 - 2015**: The ESP8266 gained widespread adoption thanks to the open availability of software development tools (SDKs) that allowed developers to easily create custom firmware.
- **ESP32 Release Timeline**:

- 2016: Espressif Systems launched the **ESP32**, which was developed as a more powerful successor to the ESP8266. It included enhanced features like dual-core processing, Bluetooth connectivity, and improved power efficiency.
- **Late 2016 - 2017**: The ESP32 quickly caught the attention of developers and IoT enthusiasts, largely due to its increased processing power and additional features.

Timeline of Hardware Updates and Firmware Improvements

- **ESP8266 Hardware and Firmware Evolution**:
  - **2014**: The initial version of ESP8266 had limited software support and was primarily used in basic Wi-Fi-enabled projects.
  - **2015 - 2016**: Espressif improved SDK support, adding more stable and feature-rich firmware. This enabled developers to take advantage of better Wi-Fi stability, power management, and the ability to customize applications.
  - **NodeMCU Boards**: Popular third-party development boards, like NodeMCU, made ESP8266 more accessible by adding USB connectivity, voltage regulators, and breakout pins.

- **ESP32 Hardware and Firmware Evolution**:
  - **2016**: The first ESP32 modules, like the ESP-WROOM-32, were released. They included new features such as Bluetooth Low Energy (BLE) and multiple analog and digital peripherals.
  - **2017 - 2018**: Firmware updates focused on improving Bluetooth stack performance, reducing power consumption, and optimizing GPIO and I/O functions.
  - **New Variants**: Different versions of the ESP32 module have been introduced to cater to specific needs, such as the **ESP32-S2** (targeted towards

security-sensitive applications) and **ESP32-C3** (based on the RISC-V architecture for cost-effective solutions).

ESP8266 to ESP32: The Evolution

Reasons for the Development of ESP32

The **ESP8266** was revolutionary for making Wi-Fi connectivity affordable, but it had some limitations, which led to the development of the **ESP32**. Key reasons for this evolution include:

- **Enhanced Processing Power**: The ESP8266 has a single-core processor with limited power, which restricts its multitasking capabilities. The ESP32 was developed with **dual-core processors** to provide more power for handling multiple tasks efficiently.
- **Additional Connectivity Options**: While the ESP8266 only supported Wi-Fi, the ESP32 introduced **Bluetooth** and **Bluetooth Low Energy (BLE)** capabilities, enabling a wider range of connectivity options.
- **Power Efficiency**: One key drawback of the ESP8266 was its relatively high power consumption for battery-operated applications. The ESP32 offers **low-power modes** and better power management, making it suitable for portable devices..

Enhancements Over ESP8266

The **ESP32** includes several significant improvements over the **ESP8266**:

- **More GPIO Pins**: The ESP32 features more GPIO pins, which provides greater flexibility in connecting peripherals, sensors, and other hardware.

- **Dual-Core Processor**: Unlike the single-core ESP8266, the ESP32 features a **dual-core Xtensa LX6 processor**, which enables better multitasking and overall performance.
- **Built-in Peripherals**: The ESP32 comes with a host of built-in peripherals, such as **analog-to-digital converters (ADCs)**, **capacitive touch sensors**, **temperature sensors**, and even **digital-to-analog converters (DACs)**.
- **Multiple Communication Interfaces**: The ESP32 supports **SPI, I2C, UART**, and **CAN**, allowing for more versatile communication between components.

Impact on IoT Community

How ESP8266 Revolutionised Affordable Wi-Fi Modules

The **ESP8266** marked a revolutionary shift in the IoT community by significantly reducing the cost of adding Wi-Fi capabilities to electronic devices. Before the ESP8266, Wi-Fi modules were often costly, making it impractical for smaller projects or DIY enthusiasts. Key impacts of the ESP8266 include:

- **Lowered Barriers to Entry**: The low cost and ease of use of the ESP8266 democratized access to Wi-Fi-enabled microcontrollers, making them accessible for hobbyists, students, and developers on a budget.
- **Community and Ecosystem Growth**: The availability of open-source SDKs and extensive community support helped foster a large and engaged developer base. This resulted in the rapid growth of tutorials, libraries, and projects that further popularized the module.
- **Rise of DIY IoT Projects**: ESP8266 enabled the development of countless **DIY projects**, such as smart lights, Wi-Fi weather stations, and connected sensors, inspiring more people to engage in IoT development.

The Adoption of ESP32 in Advanced IoT Applications

The **ESP32** took the success of the ESP8266 a step further by introducing features that made it suitable for more advanced IoT applications:

- **Complex Applications**: With its **dual-core processing, Bluetooth**, and more GPIO options, the ESP32 is commonly used in complex projects such as **robotics, real-time monitoring systems**, and **wearables**.
- **Industrial IoT**: The increased power and versatility of the ESP32 have also made it a popular choice in industrial IoT (IIoT) applications, such as remote monitoring, data logging, and automation systems.
- **Expanded Use Cases**: Bluetooth and Bluetooth Low Energy (BLE) support have allowed the ESP32 to be used in projects that require device-to-device communication, such as **smart health** devices, **home automation**, and **mesh networks**.

Future of ESP32 and ESP8266 in IoT

Future of ESP8266

- **Continued Use in Basic IoT Projects**: Given its affordability, the **ESP8266** is likely to remain a popular choice for basic IoT projects that do not require high processing power or Bluetooth. It will continue to be used by beginners and makers looking to create simple, internet-connected devices.
- **Educational Use**: The ESP8266 will remain an educational tool for learning about IoT and microcontrollers. Its simplicity makes it an ideal choice for introducing students and new developers to Wi-Fi-based projects.

Future of ESP32

- **Expanded Industrial Applications**: With its robust processing capabilities and connectivity options, the **ESP32** will continue to be adopted in more advanced industrial applications and environments where more reliable and flexible connectivity is needed.

- **Growing Integration with AI and Machine Learning**: As AI and edge computing become more prevalent, the ESP32, with its processing power, is well-positioned to support **machine learning models** at the edge, making it suitable for applications like **smart cameras**, **voice recognition**, and **predictive maintenance**.
- **New Variants and Features**: Espressif has continued to expand the ESP32 family with variants like **ESP32-S3** and **ESP32-C3**, each with unique features that cater to specific use cases (e.g., enhanced AI capabilities, reduced cost). This diversification ensures that the ESP32 line remains adaptable and versatile for various IoT needs.

Pinout and Hardware Layout

Understanding the pinout and hardware layout of microcontrollers like **ESP32** and **ESP8266** is essential for connecting sensors, peripherals, and other electronic components effectively. Both ESP32 and ESP8266 have different sets of pins with specific functions that define their use cases in projects.

ESP32 Pinout Diagram

The **ESP32** microcontroller comes with numerous **GPIO pins** and a variety of other specialized pins that can be used for different purposes. Here's a high-level description of the **ESP32 pinout**:

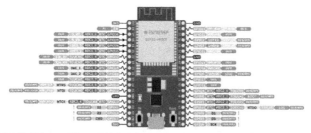

- **GPIO Pins**: The ESP32 typically has **36 GPIO pins** (depending on the variant). These pins can be used as digital inputs or outputs. Many of these pins also have additional functions, such as PWM, ADC, or touch sensors.
- **Power Pins**:
  - **3.3V Pin**: Supplies 3.3 volts of power to the board.
  - **Vin Pin**: This pin is used to power the ESP32 from an external 5V power source.
  - **Ground (GND) Pins**: Connect to the ground of the circuit.
- **Analog Input Pins (ADC)**: The ESP32 has multiple ADC pins that can be used to read analog sensors. There are **18 channels** available, with a resolution of up to **12 bits**.
- **Touch Sensors**: The ESP32 has **capacitive touch pins** (T0 to T9), allowing for touch-based input detection.
- **UART, SPI, I2C, and PWM Pins**: These pins provide communication interfaces to connect peripherals.
  - **UART**: Supports up to 3 UART interfaces for serial communication.
  - **SPI/I2C**: Multiple SPI and I2C pins allow for interfacing with sensors and other devices.
  - **PWM**: Most GPIOs can be used for **PWM** (Pulse Width Modulation), useful for controlling LEDs and motors.

- **Other Special Pins**:

○ **EN Pin**: The **Enable** pin (EN) is used to reset the microcontroller.
○ **Boot Pin (IO0)**: Used to put the ESP32 into **bootloader mode** for uploading firmware.

ESP8266 Pinout Diagram

The **ESP8266** has fewer pins compared to the ESP32, and understanding its pinout is crucial for using it effectively in simpler projects.

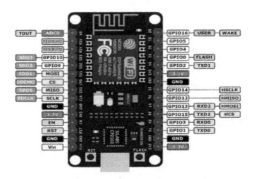

- **GPIO Pins**: The ESP8266 generally has **17 GPIO pins** available (depending on the development board). These pins serve multiple functions and can be configured as digital input or output.
- **Power Pins**:
  ○ **3.3V Pin**: Supplies power to the ESP8266 (typically operates at 3.3V).
  ○ **Vin Pin**: Powers the module with an input voltage range of 4.5V to 12V, depending on the board.
  ○ **Ground (GND) Pins**: Connects to the ground of the circuit.
- **Analog Input Pin (ADC0)**: The ESP8266 has **one analog input pin** (ADC0), which can measure voltages from 0 to 1V.
- **UART, SPI, I2C, and PWM Pins**:
  ○ **UART**: Supports serial communication for programming and debugging.

- **SPI/I2C**: Fewer communication options compared to ESP32, but SPI and I2C are still supported for external components.
- **PWM**: Limited GPIO pins can be configured for PWM, mainly for controlling simple components like LEDs.
- **CH_PD Pin**: The **Chip Power-Down** pin is used to enable or disable the chip.

Pin Functions and Description

Power Pins

- **ESP32 and ESP8266 both have 3.3V and GND pins** for power supply. It's crucial to ensure that the **input voltage** is regulated to prevent damaging the microcontrollers.
- The **Vin pin** can be used to provide external power; however, the voltage requirements for ESP32 and ESP8266 may vary slightly depending on the board.

Input/Output Pins

- Both **ESP32** and **ESP8266** GPIO pins can be configured as **inputs or outputs**, making them versatile for controlling components like LEDs, motors, or reading sensor values.
- **ESP32**: Offers **more GPIO pins** (typically 36), which allows more components to be connected simultaneously.
- **ESP8266**: Offers fewer GPIO pins (usually **17**), which can be a limitation when attempting to connect multiple peripherals.

GPIO Limitations and Considerations

- **ESP32**:
    - Not all GPIO pins are available for general use. Some pins have specific functions (e.g., flash, boot mode) and should be avoided in general-purpose use unless configured correctly.
    - Pins like **GPIO6 to GPIO11** are used for the internal flash and should **not** be used for other purposes.

- **ESP8266**:
  - **GPIO0, GPIO2, and GPIO15**: These pins have special functions during boot mode and should be used carefully to avoid conflicts during power-up.
  - **Limited Number of GPIOs**: With fewer GPIOs, you may need to use **multiplexing** techniques or **GPIO expanders** to connect additional components.

Interrupt Capabilities

- **ESP32**: Supports **interrupts** on almost all GPIO pins. This feature is crucial when you need the microcontroller to respond immediately to an event, like a button press.
- **ESP8266**: Interrupts are also supported but are more limited. Care should be taken to avoid using certain pins that may not properly support interrupts.

Analog Input Limitations

- **ESP32**:
  - The ESP32 has **multiple ADC channels** (up to 18), with a 12-bit resolution, which provides more precise analog readings.
  - However, the **ADC** is known to be **non-linear**, and calibration may be required to get accurate results.
- **ESP8266**:
  - The **ESP8266** has only **one ADC pin** (ADC0), and its range is limited to 0-1V, which can be restrictive when trying to read analog signals with higher voltages.
  - A voltage divider may be needed to bring the input voltage within the acceptable range of the ADC.

GPIO Pin Details and Usage for ESP32 and ESP8266

GPIO Pin Number	Pin Type	ESP32	ESP8266	Use
GPIO 0	Digital I/O	Yes	Yes	Boot mode selection, LED control
GPIO 1 (TX)	UART TX	Yes	Yes	Serial communication (data transmission)
GPIO 2	Digital I/O	Yes	Yes	LED control, status indication
GPIO 3 (RX)	UART RX	Yes	Yes	Serial communication (data reception)
GPIO 4	Digital I/O	Yes	Yes	General-purpose tasks, sensors, LEDs
GPIO 5	Digital I/O	Yes	Yes	Motor control, PWM
GPIO 6-11	Flash Memory	No	No	Reserved (do not use)
GPIO 12	Digital I/O	Yes	Yes	General-purpose tasks, output devices
GPIO 13	Digital I/O, PWM	Yes	Yes	LED dimming, motor control
GPIO 14	Digital I/O, PWM	Yes	Yes	PWM for motor or LED, sensor input

GPIO 15	Digital I/O, PWM	Yes	Yes	PWM, sensor or device control
GPIO 16	Digital I/O, Wake	Yes	Yes	Wake from deep sleep, low-power projects
GPIO 17	Digital I/O	Yes	No	General-purpose tasks
GPIO 18	SPI SCK	Yes	No	SPI communication (clock line)
GPIO 19	SPI MISO	Yes	No	SPI communication (data reception)
GPIO 21	I2C SDA	Yes	No	I2C communication (data line)
GPIO 22	I2C SCL	Yes	No	I2C communication (clock line)
GPIO 23	SPI MOSI	Yes	No	SPI communication (data transmission)
GPIO 25-27	Digital I/O, ADC	Yes	No	Reading analog values from sensors
GPIO 32-39	ADC	Yes	No	Analog input (e.g., sensors like LDRs)

Power Supply Requirements:

Voltage Range and Power Consumption:

- **ESP32**: The ESP32 operates within a voltage range of **3.0V to 3.6V**, with an ideal input voltage of **3.3V**. It is capable of drawing a substantial amount of current, especially during

Wi-Fi transmission. During peak usage (like Wi-Fi transmission), the ESP32 can consume around **160-240 mA**, while in idle mode, it typically consumes around **20-30 mA**.

- **ESP8266**: The ESP8266 also operates in a voltage range of **3.0V to 3.6V**, typically running at **3.3V**. Its power consumption is slightly lower than that of the ESP32, with peak currents reaching **170 mA** during Wi-Fi transmission. In idle mode, the current draw is roughly **10-20 mA**.

Power Management Hardware: Both ESP32 and ESP8266 have built-in capabilities to manage power consumption effectively:

- **Voltage Regulators**: Most development boards for the ESP32 and ESP8266 (such as NodeMCU or ESP32 DevKit) come with onboard **voltage regulators** that convert higher input voltages (like 5V from USB) to the required **3.3V** for the microcontroller. These voltage regulators ensure that the input power is within the safe operating range.
- **Decoupling Capacitors**: To ensure stable voltage supply and avoid fluctuations during peak power usage, decoupling capacitors are often included on development boards.

Battery Power and USB Power Options:

- **Battery Power**: Both ESP32 and ESP8266 can be powered using batteries, making them ideal for portable projects. Typical battery options include **Li-ion/Li-Po** batteries (3.7V nominal voltage). For battery-powered setups, a voltage regulator is necessary to step down the voltage to **3.3V**. The ESP32 is designed with several power-saving modes, making it suitable for long-term battery-powered applications.
- **USB Power**: Development boards for both ESP32 and ESP8266 generally have a **micro USB port** for powering and programming the microcontroller. The USB power supplies **5V**, which is then regulated down to **3.3V** on the board.

Current Draw During Different States:

Active Mode:

- **ESP32**: In active mode, when all components are running, including Wi-Fi, the ESP32 can consume between **160-240 mA**. This high power draw occurs primarily during transmission and data processing. The dual-core processor adds to the power requirements when both cores are in operation.
- **ESP8266**: In active mode with Wi-Fi enabled, the ESP8266 draws about **150-170 mA**. This is slightly lower compared to the ESP32 due to its simpler architecture and lower processing power.

Sleep Mode:

- **ESP32**: The ESP32 is highly optimized for low-power operation, offering several sleep modes, including **light sleep** and **deep sleep**. In **deep sleep mode**, the ESP32 can reduce its power consumption to around **10 µA**, making it suitable for battery-powered devices where long operational life is required. **Light sleep** typically uses a bit more power, around **1-5 mA**.
- **ESP8266**: The ESP8266 also offers sleep modes, although they are less sophisticated compared to the ESP32. In **deep sleep mode**, the ESP8266 can reduce power consumption to about **20 µA**, which is higher than the ESP32. The wake-up process from deep sleep is relatively slower, which may affect its use in some applications requiring quick responses.

Development Environment and Getting Started

Programming Platforms:

Arduino IDE: The **Arduino IDE** is one of the most beginner-friendly environments for programming both the **ESP32** and **ESP8266**. It provides a simplified interface with numerous examples and libraries that make it easy to get started.

- To use ESP32 or ESP8266 with Arduino IDE, you need to add support by going to **File > Preferences**, then adding the board manager URL for ESP:
  - **ESP32**:

```
https://dl.espressif.com/dl/package_esp32_index.json
```

  - **ESP8266**:

```
http://arduino.esp8266.com/stable/package_esp8266com_index.json
```

- Once added, you can install the board package via **Tools > Board > Boards Manager** and select the appropriate board for your project.

ESP-IDF (Espressif IoT Development Framework): **ESP-IDF** is the official development framework for the **ESP32** and is more suited for advanced users who want more control over the hardware.

- It provides a comprehensive set of libraries and tools, supporting advanced features such as dual-core operation, Wi-Fi, and Bluetooth configurations.
- Setting up ESP-IDF involves installing the toolchain, Python dependencies, and setting up environment variables. It provides more flexibility and is suitable for professionals working on production-level projects.

MicroPython: **MicroPython** is a popular option for those who prefer scripting over compiled code. It is ideal for rapid prototyping, and both the **ESP32** and **ESP8266** support MicroPython.

- MicroPython can be flashed onto the device, allowing you to write Python scripts to interact with the hardware. It's a great option for beginners who already have some familiarity with Python programming.
- Tools like **Thonny** or **uPyCraft** IDEs make it easy to connect to and program MicroPython on ESP modules.

Required Hardware and Tools:

USB-to-Serial Converter: Most **ESP32** and **ESP8266** development boards, like NodeMCU and ESP32 DevKit, come with a built-in USB-to-serial converter, allowing easy connection to your computer via USB. For standalone modules (e.g., ESP-12 or ESP-01), an external **USB-to-Serial converter** (e.g., **CP2102** or **FTDI232**) is required for flashing and communication.

Power Supply Modules: For reliable operation, a **power supply module** is often needed to provide a stable **3.3V** supply. This can be achieved via:

- **USB Power**: The development boards can be powered through a USB cable.
- **Battery Power**: **Li-ion/Li-Po** batteries are commonly used, especially for portable projects.

Setting Up Development Environment for Multiple OS:

Windows Setup:

1. Install **Arduino IDE** and add ESP32 or ESP8266 board support through the **Boards Manager**.
2. Install the necessary **USB drivers** (e.g., **CP2102** or **CH340** drivers) for Windows to recognize the board.
3. For **ESP-IDF**, download and install the ESP-IDF Tools Installer, which will automatically set up Python, Git, and other dependencies.

macOS Setup:

1. Download and install **Arduino IDE**.
2. Use the macOS **Board Manager URL** to add ESP32 or ESP8266 support.
3. Install **Homebrew** for additional dependencies and install drivers using *brew install*.

4. Set up **ESP-IDF** by following Espressif's installation guide for macOS, which includes setting up Git and Python dependencies.

Linux Setup:

1. Install **Arduino IDE** from the official website and add the required board manager URLs.
2. Linux usually has most USB drivers built-in, but additional permissions might be required to access the serial ports (*/dev/ttyUSB0* or */dev/ttyAMA0*). You may need to add your user to the **dialout** group: *sudo usermod -a -G dialout $USER*
3. Install the **ESP-IDF** by following the official Linux installation guide, which includes installing necessary dependencies via package managers like **apt**.

Basic Troubleshooting for Setup (Driver Issues, Flashing Problems):

Driver Issues:

- If your computer does not recognize the ESP32 or ESP8266, you may need to install drivers for **USB-to-Serial chips** like **CP2102**, **CH340**, or **FTDI**.
- Ensure that the correct COM port is selected in the **Arduino IDE** under **Tools > Port**.

Flashing Problems:

- **Common Errors**: "Failed to connect to ESP32" is a common error when the microcontroller is not in bootloader mode. Press and hold the **BOOT** button while uploading code to put the ESP32 in flashing mode.
- Ensure the **baud rate** is set correctly (usually *115200*).

Flashing Firmware:

Using ESP-Tool to Flash:

- **ESP-Tool** is a command-line utility provided by Espressif for flashing firmware onto ESP32 and ESP8266 devices.
- **Installation**: Install `esptool` using Python's package manager: *pip install esptool*
- **Usage**: Connect your ESP board and run the following command to erase the flash memory: *esptool.py erase_flash* To flash new firmware: *esptool.py --port COM3 write_flash -z 0x0000 firmware.bin* Replace *COM3* with the appropriate port (e.g., */dev/ttyUSB0* on Linux) and *firmware.bin* with the path to your firmware file.

Troubleshooting Common Issues:

USB Connectivity Problems (Beyond Initial Setup): Even after setting up the initial development environment, you might encounter USB connectivity issues:

- **USB Port Not Recognized**:
  - *Check USB Cable*: Some USB cables are power-only and do not support data transfer. Make sure you are using a **data-capable USB cable**.
  - *Port Selection*: Ensure the correct **COM port** is selected in the **Arduino IDE** under **Tools > Port**.
  - *Reinstall Drivers*: Sometimes, drivers may become corrupted. Reinstalling drivers for **CP2102**, **CH340**, or **FTDI** can help resolve recognition issues.
- **Board Keeps Disconnecting**:
  - *Power Supply Issue*: Ensure that the board is receiving stable power. A poor-quality USB cable or insufficient power from the USB port can cause disconnections. Using a powered USB hub can provide a more stable power supply.
  - *USB Port Overload*: Avoid plugging multiple power-consuming devices into the same USB hub as your ESP board, as this may cause voltage drops, resulting in random disconnections.

Wi-Fi Connectivity Issues:

- **Unable to Connect to Wi-Fi**:
  - *Wrong Credentials*: Double-check the **SSID** and **password**. Simple typos can lead to connection failures.
  - *Wi-Fi Signal Strength*: Place the ESP module closer to the router or access point, and ensure there aren't many obstacles. Use the **WiFi.RSSI()** function in **Arduino IDE** or similar methods to check signal strength.
  - *Channel Overcrowding*: Many Wi-Fi networks on the same channel can cause interference. If possible, change the router's channel to a less crowded one.
- **Intermittent Wi-Fi Disconnection**:
  - *Power Supply Stability*: Ensure a stable power supply, as Wi-Fi transmission draws significant current. Voltage fluctuations can cause the microcontroller to reset or disconnect from Wi-Fi.
  - *Firmware Update*: Older firmware may have issues maintaining a stable Wi-Fi connection. Updating to the latest **ESP32** or **ESP8266 firmware** can resolve such issues.

Debugging Tools and Techniques:

- **Serial Monitor**:
  - The **Serial Monitor** in **Arduino IDE** is a fundamental tool for debugging. Use *Serial.print()* statements to understand the flow of your code and identify where errors occur.
- **Logic Analyzers**:
  - For communication issues (such as **I2C** or **SPI**), a **logic analyzer** can help you understand what data is being transmitted and identify where errors might be occurring.

- **ESP-IDF Monitor**:
  - If using **ESP-IDF**, the integrated **ESP-IDF Monitor** provides useful logs and real-time debugging information. It is especially useful for understanding deeper issues like crashes or stack traces.

Best Practices for Using ESP32/ESP8266:

Power Supply Stability:

- Ensure a **reliable 3.3V power supply**. Both ESP32 and ESP8266 can draw spikes of current during Wi-Fi transmissions. If you are using a linear regulator, make sure it can handle at least **500 mA** of current.
- When using battery power, consider a **Li-Po battery** with a **DC-DC buck converter** to ensure stable voltage, as voltage drops can cause unexpected reboots.

Proper GPIO Usage:

- **ESP32**: Not all GPIO pins are available for general use, as some are used internally by the microcontroller (e.g., for flash or boot). Avoid using **GPIO6 to GPIO11** for other purposes, as these are connected to the integrated flash memory.
- **ESP8266**: Special GPIO pins like **GPIO0**, **GPIO2**, and **GPIO15** are involved in the boot process. Ensure proper connections if these pins are used, as incorrect connections can cause the board to not boot correctly.
- Use **current-limiting resistors** (typically **220 ohms to 1k ohms**) when connecting LEDs or other components to GPIO pins to protect both the pins and external components.

Antenna Placement for Wi-Fi:

- **Avoid Obstacles**: The onboard antenna should not be obstructed by metal components, power supplies, or other electronics that could interfere with signal transmission.

- **Distance from Power Sources**: Place the ESP module away from power supplies, as electromagnetic interference can degrade Wi-Fi performance.
- **Proper Orientation**: The onboard PCB antenna is directional. Make sure the module is oriented so that the antenna faces outward for optimal coverage.

Chapter-2 Variables and data types

In this chapter, we explore various data types used in Arduino programming for ESP32 and ESP8266 microcontrollers. Data types are essential building blocks for any program as they determine the kind of data a variable can store. We will discuss basic data types like integers, floats, characters, and booleans, as well as more advanced types like unsigned integers, long integers, double-precision floats, strings, and arrays. Understanding how to use these data types effectively will help you write efficient and memory-conscious programs on resource-constrained microcontrollers like the ESP32/ESP8266.

Syntax Table

Topics	Syntax	Simple Example
Integer (int)	int variableName = value;	int ledPin = 13;
Float (float)	float variableName = value;	float temperature = 23.5;
Character (char)	char variableName = 'character';	char myChar = 'A';
Boolean (bool)	bool variableName = true;	bool ledState = false;

Unsigned Integer (unsigned int)	unsigned int variableName = value;	unsigned int distance = 1500;
Long (long)	long variableName = value;	long population = 7000000000;
Unsigned Long (unsigned long)	unsigned long variableName = value;	unsigned long startTime = millis();
Double (double)	double variableName = value;	double preciseValue = 0.000123456;
String Object (String)	String variableName = "text";	String greeting = "Hello World";
C-style String (char array)	char variableName[] = "text";	char greeting[] = "Hello World";
Array	dataType arrayName[arraySize];	int sensorValues[5] = {10, 20, 30, 40, 50};

1. Basic Data Types

Integer (int):

An integer is a data type used to represent whole numbers without decimals. It is commonly used for counting, indexing, or specifying fixed values like pin numbers.

Why is Important
Integers are essential for efficient memory usage, especially on microcontrollers like the ESP32/ESP8266 where resources are limited. They are perfect for storing whole numbers, making them useful for tasks like loop counters, digital pin control, and state management.

Syntax

```
int variableName = value;
```

Syntax Explanation

- *int*: Declares the variable as an integer type.
- *variableName*: The name of the integer variable.
- *value*: The whole number to assign to the variable.

Code Example

```
int ledPin = 13;
void setup() {
  pinMode(ledPin, OUTPUT);
}
void loop() {
  digitalWrite(ledPin, HIGH);
  delay(1000);
  digitalWrite(ledPin, LOW);
  delay(1000);

}
```

Notes

- An integer on the ESP32/ESP8266 is 16-bit and takes up 2 bytes of memory.
- Use integers for whole number operations like counting or storing pin numbers.

Warnings

- Be cautious of overflow; exceeding the integer range of -32,768 to 32,767 will result in unexpected behavior.

Float (float):

A float is a data type that represents numbers with decimal points, such as 3.14 or -7.25. This allows you to store and work with numbers that have a fractional component, which is crucial for precise calculations.

Why is Important

Floats are important when your program needs to handle values that aren't whole numbers. For example, sensor readings (like temperature, distance, or humidity) often produce decimal numbers. Using floats allows you to capture and process these values accurately.

Syntax

```
float variableName = value;
```

Syntax Explanation

- *float*: Declares the variable as a float type.
- *variableName*: The name you choose for the variable.
- *value*: The decimal number you assign to the variable.

Code Example

```
float temperature = 23.5;
void setup() {
  Serial.begin(9600);
}
void loop() {
  Serial.println(temperature);
  temperature += 0.1;
  delay(1000);
}
```

Notes

- On the ESP32/ESP8266, a float takes up 4 bytes of memory.
- Use floats for calculations that require decimal precision, such as sensor data or physics simulations.

Warnings

- Floats take more memory and processing power compared to integers, so use them only when necessary.
- Floats can sometimes produce small rounding errors due to the way they're stored, so be careful when comparing them.

Character (char):

A character (char) is a data type that stores a single character, like a letter, digit, or symbol. It can also store the corresponding ASCII value of that character. For example, 'A' has an ASCII value of 65.

Why is Important
Chars are useful when working with text or characters in a program. They allow you to handle single characters or work with ASCII values, which are commonly used in embedded systems for communication and data manipulation.

Syntax

```
char variableName = 'character';
```

Syntax Explanation

- *char*: Declares the variable as a character type.
- *variableName*: The name of the character variable.
- *'character'*: The single character to be stored, enclosed in single quotes.

Code Example

```
char myChar = 'A';
void setup() {
  Serial.begin(9600);
}
void loop() {
  Serial.println(myChar);
  delay(1000);
}
```

Notes

- A char on the ESP32/ESP8266 uses 1 byte of memory.
- Chars can store any valid ASCII character, including letters, digits, and symbols.

Warnings

- Chars can only store one character at a time. If you need to store multiple characters, use a string or character array.
- Make sure the character is enclosed in single quotes (') when assigning a value.

Boolean (bool):

Boolean (bool) is a data type in Arduino that stores values representing either **true** or **false**. This data type is crucial in decision-making processes and logic controls, especially in conditions like *if* statements.

Why is Important?
Booleans are essential for creating control structures in programming. They are commonly used in conditions, loops, and logic checks, allowing your ESP32/ESP8266 code to respond to certain conditions and make decisions during execution.

Syntax

```
bool variableName = true;
```

Syntax Explanation

- *bool* declares the variable as a Boolean type.
- *variableName* is the name of your variable.
- *true* or *false* is the value assigned to the variable.

Code Example

```
bool ledState = false;
if (digitalRead(2) == HIGH) {
ledState = true;
}
```

Notes

- Booleans take only **1 byte** of memory, making them memory-efficient.
- Boolean values can only be **true** or **false**, no other values.

Warnings

- Avoid using integers like *1* and *0* as Boolean substitutes directly; although *1* may be interpreted as **true** and *0* as **false**, it's good practice to stick to the actual **true** and **false** values for clarity and maintainability.

2. Advanced Data Types

Unsigned Integer (`unsigned int`):

An unsigned integer (*unsigned int*) is a data type in Arduino that stores only positive whole numbers, ranging from **0 to 65,535**. This is different from a regular integer, which can store both negative and positive numbers.

Why is Important?
Unsigned int is crucial when you need to store values that will never be negative, allowing you to make full use of the available memory. It is especially useful for counting, timing, or handling data where negative values are not logical or necessary.

Syntax

```
unsigned int variableName = 100;
```

Syntax Explanation

- *unsigned int* declares the variable as an unsigned integer type.
- *variableName* is the name of your variable.
- *100* is an example of a positive number assigned to the variable.

Code Example

```
unsigned int distance = 1500;
if (distance > 1000) {
Serial.println("Long distance");
}
```

Notes

- Unsigned integers take **2 bytes** of memory, which allows them to store values from **0 to 65,535**.
- They are great for counting values like time intervals, sensor readings, and other data that can only be positive.

Warnings

- If you try to assign a negative value to an *unsigned int*, the result will be incorrect, as unsigned integers cannot represent negative numbers. Be mindful of the value ranges while working with them.

Long (long):

A *long* is a data type in Arduino that stores larger whole numbers, typically ranging from **-2,147,483,648 to 2,147,483,647**. It provides a wider range than a regular *int* type, allowing you to handle bigger numbers in your code.

Why is Important?

The *long* data type is crucial when you need to work with large numbers that exceed the limits of an *int*. It's commonly used for scenarios like timing, counting large values, or any situation where integers may not be enough to store the desired range of data.

Syntax

```
long variableName = 100000;
```

Syntax Explanation

- *long* declares the variable as a long integer type.
- *variableName* is the name of your variable.
- *100000* is an example of a large number assigned to the variable.

Code Example

```
long population = 7000000000;
if (population > 6000000000) {
Serial.println("The world is growing!");
}
```

Notes

- A *long* takes **4 bytes** of memory and can store larger numbers compared to an *int*, which is why it is used when higher limits are required.
- The *long* data type is signed, meaning it can store both positive and negative numbers.

Warnings

- Be cautious when using *long* variables if your application does not require such large numbers, as they consume more memory compared to *int*.

Unsigned Long (`unsigned long`):

Unsigned long is a data type in Arduino that stores only positive long numbers, ranging from **0 to 4,294,967,295**. It is often used to track time in milliseconds, especially when using functions like *millis()*.

Why is Important?
Unsigned long is crucial when dealing with very large numbers that are always positive, such as timing functions, long delays, or sensor readings that require more than the limits of a regular *int*. The ability to store large values is particularly useful for timekeeping over long periods.

Syntax

```
unsigned long variableName = 500000;
```

Syntax Explanation

- *unsigned long* declares the variable as an unsigned long integer type.
- *variableName* is the name of your variable.
- *500000* is an example of a positive number assigned to the variable.

Code Example

```
unsigned long startTime = millis();
if (millis() - startTime > 1000) {
Serial.println("One second has passed");
}
```

Notes

- An *unsigned long* takes **4 bytes** of memory and can only store positive values.
- It is frequently used for time-tracking purposes using *millis()* or *micros()* in Arduino, which return the number of milliseconds or microseconds since the program started.

Warnings

- Be mindful of the fact that *unsigned long* variables cannot store negative values. Trying to use negative values can lead to unexpected results.

Double (`double`):

A *double* is a data type in Arduino that is similar to *float* but provides more precision for storing decimal numbers. It is particularly useful for mathematical calculations that require a higher degree of accuracy.

Why is Important?
The *double* data type is important when precision is needed in your calculations, such as in scientific computations, sensor data processing, or any situation where small differences in values are significant. Unlike *float*, *double* provides a wider range of accuracy.

Syntax

```
double variableName = 3.14159;
```

Syntax Explanation

- *double* declares the variable as a double-precision floating-point type.
- *variableName* is the name of your variable.
- *3.14159* is an example of a decimal number assigned to the variable.

Code Example

```
double preciseValue = 0.000123456;
double result = preciseValue * 1000000;
Serial.println(result);
```

Notes

- On most Arduino boards, *double* is the same as *float* and uses **4 bytes**, with 6-7 decimal digits of precision. On some platforms, like the ESP32, *double* uses **8 bytes**, offering more precision than *float*.
- Use *double* when higher precision is necessary in calculations, especially on platforms that support its extended precision.

Warnings

- Be cautious when using *double* on platforms where it has the same precision as *float*, as it may not provide the additional precision you expect. Always check the specific behavior of the platform you're working with.

3. Textual Data

String Object (`String`):

A *String* object in Arduino stores a sequence of characters, making it useful for creating and manipulating words, messages, or any text-based data (e.g., "Hello World"). It allows for easy handling of text in your code.

Why is Important?
The *String* object is important because it simplifies working with text and characters in Arduino. It allows for flexible text manipulation, such as concatenation, comparison, and extraction, which is crucial for tasks like displaying messages, handling input, or creating readable outputs.

Syntax

```
String variableName = "Hello World";
```

Syntax Explanation

- *String* declares the variable as a String object.
- *variableName* is the name of your variable.
- *"Hello World"* is an example of a string of characters assigned to the variable.

Code Example

```
String greeting = "Hello World";
Serial.println(greeting);
```

Notes

- The *String* object provides many built-in functions for manipulating text, such as *length()*, *substring()*, *concat()*, and *replace()*.
- It is easier to use than traditional character arrays (*char[]*), especially when dealing with dynamic or unknown-length strings.

Warnings

- *String* objects can consume significant memory, especially on microcontrollers with limited RAM. Be cautious when using them in memory-constrained environments like the ESP8266, as they can lead to memory fragmentation and instability.

C-style String (char array):

A *C-style String* is a character array in Arduino that stores a sequence of characters, ending with a special null character ('\0'). This null character indicates the end of the string. *C-style Strings* are more memory-efficient and are often used in memory-constrained environments.

Why is Important?
C-style Strings are important when you need a lightweight, efficient

way to handle strings, especially on devices with limited memory like the ESP8266. Unlike *String* objects, which can cause memory issues, *char arrays* are more predictable in terms of memory usage and can help avoid memory fragmentation.

Syntax

```
char variableName[] = "Hello";
```

Syntax Explanation

- *char* declares the variable as a character array.
- *variableName[]* is the name of your variable with square brackets indicating it's an array.
- *"Hello"* is an example string of characters assigned to the array, automatically terminated with the null character '\0'.

Code Example

```
char greeting[] = "Hello World";
Serial.println(greeting);
```

Notes

- A *C-style String* must always end with a null character ('\0') to indicate the end of the string.
- You can manipulate *char arrays* using functions like *strcpy()*, *strlen()*, and *strcat()* for copying, getting the length, or concatenating strings.

Warnings

- Make sure the array is large enough to hold the string and the null character. If the array size is too small, you risk buffer overflow, which can lead to unpredictable behavior or crashes.

- Unlike *String* objects, *char arrays* don't automatically resize, so you need to manage memory carefully.

4. Array

Array:

An *array* in Arduino is a collection of elements, all of the same type, stored under one variable name. It allows you to store multiple values, like numbers or sensor readings, in a single variable. For example, *int sensorValues[5]* lets you store five integer values.

Why is Important?
Arrays are important because they help you manage multiple related values efficiently. Instead of creating a separate variable for each sensor reading or value, you can group them into an array. This makes your code simpler, easier to read, and more organized, especially when working with multiple data points like sensors.

Syntax

```
dataType arrayName[arraySize];
```

Syntax Explanation

- *dataType* tells the type of values the array will store (e.g., *int*, *float*).
- *arrayName* is the name of the array.
- *arraySize* is the number of elements the array can hold. This size is fixed when the array is created.

Code Example

```
int sensorValues[5] = {10, 20, 30, 40, 50};
for (int i = 0; i < 5; i++) {
Serial.println(sensorValues[i]);
}
```

Notes

- Arrays in Arduino start at index 0. This means the first element is *sensorValues[0]*, the second is *sensorValues[1]*, and so on.
- The size of an array must be defined at the start and cannot be changed while your program is running.

Warnings

- Be careful not to access an element outside the array's size. For example, trying to access *sensorValues[5]* when the array only has 5 elements (0 to 4) can cause crashes or unexpected behavior.
- Arrays take up memory, so avoid using large arrays on memory-limited devices like the ESP8266, as it can cause memory issues.

Project:

1. LED State Control with Arduino ESP32/ESP8266

Control and display the state of an LED using a boolean variable, where *true* represents the LED being on, and *false* represents it being off. Instead of using an actual LED, the Serial Monitor will display the LED state based on the value stored in the variable.

Requirement:

- ESP32 or ESP8266 board
- Arduino IDE

Circuit Connection:

- No physical circuit required for this project since we will use the Serial Monitor to simulate the LED state.

Circuit Analysis:

- The GPIO pin functionality is not used in this example. Instead, the code will output the "LED" state (on or off) directly to the Serial Monitor.

How it works:

1. A boolean variable (*ledState*) will be defined in the code.
2. If *ledState* = *true*, the Serial Monitor will print "LED is ON".
3. If *ledState* = *false*, the Serial Monitor will print "LED is OFF".
4. The code will allow easy modification of the LED state by changing the value of *ledState*.

Code:

```
boolean ledState = false;
void setup() {
    Serial.begin(115200);
}
void loop() {
    if (ledState == true) {
        Serial.println("LED is ON");
    } else {
        Serial.println("LED is OFF");
    }
    delay(1000);
    ledState = !ledState;
}
```

Code Walkthrough:

- *boolean ledState = false;* defines the initial state of the "LED" as off.
- *Serial.begin(115200);* initializes serial communication.
- In the *loop()*, it checks the value of *ledState*. If it is *true*, the Serial Monitor will display *"LED is ON"*. If it is *false*, it will display *"LED is OFF"*.
- The *delay(1000);* introduces a 1-second delay between each state change.
- Finally, *ledState = !ledState;* toggles the value of *ledState*, switching between on and off.

Note:

This code is beginner-friendly and eliminates the need for physical hardware. You can easily track the LED's simulated state using the Serial Monitor in the Arduino IDE.

2. Counter with Integer for Arduino ESP32/ESP8266

Create a counter using an *int* variable that can be manually incremented or decremented in the code. The counter value will be displayed in the Serial Monitor.

Requirement:

- ESP32 or ESP8266 board
- Arduino IDE

Circuit Connection:

- No physical circuit is needed for this project. The Serial Monitor will be used to display the counter value.

Circuit Analysis:

- The code will use an *int* variable to store the counter value.
- The counter will be incremented and decremented within the loop, and the updated value will be printed to the Serial Monitor.

How it works:

1. An *int* variable (*counter*) will be defined in the code.
2. The *counter* will start at an initial value (e.g., 0).
3. The value of *counter* will be incremented and then decremented inside the loop.
4. The Serial Monitor will display the current value of *counter*.

Code:

```
int counter = 0;
void setup() {
    Serial.begin(115200);
}
void loop() {
    counter++;
    Serial.print("Counter value: ");
    Serial.println(counter);
    delay(1000);
    counter--;
    Serial.print("Counter value: ");
    Serial.println(counter);
    delay(1000);
```

```
}
```

Code Walkthrough:

- *int counter = 0;* initializes the counter.
- *Serial.begin(115200);* starts the serial communication.
- Inside the *loop()*, the counter is incremented with *counter++*, and the value is printed. After a 1-second delay, the counter is decremented with *counter--*, and the value is printed again.

Note:

This project is simple and beginner-friendly. It uses an *int* variable to track a counter, with the updated values displayed in the Serial Monitor.

3. Message Storage with String for Arduino ESP32/ESP8266

Store a predefined message in a *String* variable. Display this message in the Serial Monitor, showing how data can be stored and manipulated in string form.

Requirement:

- ESP32 or ESP8266 board
- Arduino IDE

Circuit Connection:

- No physical circuit is needed for this project. The Serial Monitor will be used to display the stored message.

Circuit Analysis:

- The code will use a *String* variable to store the message.
- The message will be displayed in the Serial Monitor.

How it works:

1. A *String* variable (*message*) will be defined in the code.
2. The *message* will hold a predefined text.
3. The text will be displayed in the Serial Monitor using the *Serial.println()* function.

Code:

```
String message = "Hello, welcome to ESP32/ESP8266 programming!";
void setup() {
    Serial.begin(115200);
    Serial.println(message);
}
void loop() {
}
```

Code Walkthrough:

- *String message = "Hello, welcome to ESP32/ESP8266 programming!";* stores a predefined message.
- *Serial.begin(115200);* initializes serial communication.
- *Serial.println(message);* outputs the message to the Serial Monitor in the *setup()* function.

Note:

This simple project demonstrates how to store and display text data using a *String* variable in Arduino. It's a fundamental example of string manipulation for beginners using the ESP32/ESP8266.

Chapter Summary

In this chapter, we covered various data types used in Arduino programming for ESP32 and ESP8266:

- **Basic Data Types**:
    - **Integer (int)**: Stores whole numbers, ideal for tasks like counting and controlling pin states.
    - **Float (float)**: Stores numbers with decimal points, suitable for precise sensor readings.
    - **Character (char)**: Stores single characters, including ASCII values, useful for text-based data.

- o **Boolean (bool)**: Stores true or false values, essential for conditions and logic in the code.
- **Advanced Data Types**:
  - o **Unsigned Integer (unsigned int)**: Stores only positive numbers, useful for values like timers or counts that should not be negative.
  - o **Long (long)**: Stores larger whole numbers, which are required when int is insufficient for big values.
  - o **Unsigned Long (unsigned long)**: Stores only positive long values, perfect for time tracking using functions like `millis()`.
  - o **Double (double)**: Stores numbers with greater precision compared to floats, useful for high-accuracy calculations.
  - o **String Object (String)**: A convenient way to handle and manipulate text in the program.
  - o **C-style String (char array)**: A more memory-efficient way to store text, often used in resource-constrained devices.
  - o **Array**: Used to store a collection of elements of the same type, making it easy to manage related values like sensor readings.

Understanding these data types and their proper usage is crucial for efficient programming in resource-constrained environments like ESP32 and ESP8266. Each data type has specific memory requirements, and selecting the appropriate type for each task ensures that your program runs efficiently and remains within the limits of the available hardware resources.

Chapter-3 Control Structures

Control structures are fundamental in Arduino programming as they help control the flow of your code. They allow your program to make decisions, repeat blocks of code, and handle specific scenarios based on conditions. This chapter covers various types of control structures used in ESP32/ESP8266 programming, including **Conditional Statements**, **Looping Structures**, **Branching Statements**, **Switch Statements**, and **Error Handling** (available in the ESP-IDF environment). Learning these structures will enable you to create dynamic, efficient, and responsive programs.

Syntax Table

Topics	Syntax	Simple Example
If Statement (if)	if (condition) { // code }	if (sensorValue > 500) { Serial.println("High!"); }
If-Else Statement (if-else)	if (condition) { // code } else { // code }	if (sensorValue > 500) { Serial.println("High!"); } else { Serial.println("Low."); }
Else-If Ladder (if-else if)	if (condition1) { // code } else if (condition2) { // code } else { // code }	if (value > 800) { Serial.println("Very High"); } else if (value > 500) { Serial.println("High"); } else { Serial.println("Low"); }
For Loop (for)	for (init; condition; increment) { // code }	for (int i = 0; i < 5; i++) { Serial.println(i); }

While Loop (while)	while (condition) { // code }	while (sensorValue < 500) { Serial.println("Waiting"); sensorValue = analogRead(A0); }
Do-While Loop (do-while)	do { // code } while (condition);	int i = 0; do { Serial.println(i); i++; } while (i < 5);
Break Statement (break)	break;	for (int i = 0; i < 10; i++) { if (i == 5) { break; } }
Continue Statement (continue)	continue;	for (int i = 0; i < 10; i++) { if (i % 2 == 0) { continue; } Serial.println(i); }
Switch Statement (switch)	switch (variable) { case value: // code; break; ... default: // code }	int mode = 2; switch (mode) { case 1: Serial.println("Mode 1"); break; case 2: Serial.println("Mode 2"); break; }
Try-Catch (ESP-IDF)	try { // code } catch (exception) { // error code }	try { readFile("/data.txt"); } catch (FileNotFoundException e) { Serial.println("File not found!"); }

1. Conditional Statements

If Statement (if)

An *if* statement in Arduino is a conditional structure that runs a block of code only when a specified condition is true. If the condition evaluates to false, the code inside the *if* block is skipped.

Why is Important?

The *if* statement is important because it allows your program to make decisions. You can control what actions your code performs based on real-time conditions, such as sensor readings, user inputs, or status changes. It helps make your program responsive to changes in its environment.

Syntax

```
if (condition) {
// code to execute if condition is true
}
```

Syntax Explanation

- *if* initiates the conditional statement.
- *(condition)* is a logical expression that evaluates to either true or false.
- The code inside the curly brackets *{}* is executed only if the condition is true.

Code Example

```
int sensorValue = analogRead(A0);
if (sensorValue > 500) {
Serial.println("Sensor value is high!");
}
```

Notes

- You can chain multiple *if* statements with *else if* and *else* for more complex decision-making.
- Conditions can use comparison operators like ==, !=, >, <, >=, and <= to evaluate the relationship between values.

Warnings

- Ensure the condition in your *if* statement is logically sound, as incorrect conditions can lead to unexpected behavior.

- Be careful when using *if* statements inside loops, as excessive conditions can slow down your program if not optimized.

If-Else Statement (if-else):

An *if-else* statement in Arduino is a conditional structure that runs one block of code if the specified condition is true, and a different block of code if the condition is false. This allows the program to choose between two actions based on a condition.

Why is Important?
The *if-else* statement is important because it enables decision-making with alternate outcomes. It provides flexibility in controlling program flow by allowing the execution of one set of instructions when a condition is true and another when it's false. This is useful in scenarios like responding to different sensor values, user input, or system states.

Syntax

```
if (condition) {
// code to execute if condition is true
} else {
// code to execute if condition is false
}
```

Syntax Explanation

- *if* starts the conditional check.
- *(condition)* is a logical expression that evaluates to either true or false.
- The code inside the first set of curly brackets *{}* executes if the condition is true.
- *else* defines the alternative block of code, which runs if the condition is false.

Code Example

```
int sensorValue = analogRead(A0);
if (sensorValue > 500) {
Serial.println("Sensor value is high!");
} else {
Serial.println("Sensor value is low.");
}
```

Notes

- The *else* block is optional; if you don't need alternative behavior, just use an *if* statement.
- You can extend decision-making further by using *else if* to check multiple conditions in sequence.

Warnings

- Ensure the logic of your *if-else* conditions covers all possible scenarios to avoid unexpected behavior.
- Avoid deeply nesting *if-else* statements, as it can make the code hard to read and debug.

Else-If Ladder (if-else if):

An *else-if* ladder in Arduino is a series of *if-else if* statements that evaluate multiple conditions in sequence. The code block for the first condition that evaluates to true is executed, and the rest of the conditions are ignored.

Why is Important?
The *else-if* ladder is important for scenarios where you need to check multiple conditions one after another. It allows you to handle various outcomes based on different conditions in a structured way. For example, it can be useful when comparing sensor readings to predefined thresholds or handling different modes of operation.

Syntax

```
if (condition1) {
// code to execute if condition1 is true
} else if (condition2) {
// code to execute if condition2 is true
} else {
```

```
// code to execute if none of the conditions are true
}
```

Syntax Explanation

- *if* initiates the first condition check.
- *(condition1)* is the first logical expression that is checked.
- If *condition1* is false, *else if* checks the next condition *(condition2)*.
- The code inside the curly brackets *{}* after the first true condition is executed, and the rest are skipped.
- The optional *else* block runs if none of the conditions are true.

Code Example

```
int sensorValue = analogRead(A0);
if (sensorValue > 800) {
Serial.println("Very High");
} else if (sensorValue > 500) {
Serial.println("High");
} else if (sensorValue > 200) {
Serial.println("Medium");
} else {
Serial.println("Low");
}
```

Notes

- Only the first condition that evaluates to true will have its code block executed. Once a true condition is found, the rest are skipped.
- You can use as many *else if* conditions as needed to handle multiple scenarios.

Warnings

- Avoid using too many conditions in a single *else-if* ladder, as it can make the code complex and harder to read.

- Ensure that each condition is mutually exclusive or in the correct sequence to prevent unexpected outcomes.

2. Looping Structures

For Loop (for):

A *for* loop in Arduino is a control structure that repeats a block of code a set number of times. It is especially useful when you know beforehand how many times the code needs to run, such as when iterating over an array or controlling a sequence of actions.

Why is Important?
The *for* loop is important because it simplifies repetitive tasks. Instead of writing the same code multiple times, a *for* loop allows you to run the code repeatedly with different values or actions on each iteration. It is commonly used for tasks like reading sensors in a loop, controlling LEDs, or processing arrays.

Syntax

```
for (initialization; condition; increment) {
// code to execute
}
```

Syntax Explanation

- *initialization* sets the starting value of the loop control variable (e.g., *int i = 0*).
- *condition* is a logical expression that must be true for the loop to continue running (e.g., *i < 10*).
- *increment* updates the control variable after each iteration (e.g., *i++*).
- The code inside the curly brackets *{}* runs on each iteration of the loop until the condition becomes false.

Code Example

```
for (int i = 0; i < 5; i++) {
Serial.println(i);
}
```

Notes

- A *for* loop is useful when the number of iterations is known or can be determined beforehand.
- It is commonly used with arrays or when performing repetitive actions like turning LEDs on and off or reading sensor values multiple times.

Warnings

- Ensure the condition in the loop is correct to avoid infinite loops, which can cause your program to get stuck.
- Be cautious with the *increment* part of the loop, as incorrect updates can lead to the loop never terminating or skipping iterations unexpectedly.

While Loop (while):

A *while* loop in Arduino is a control structure that repeatedly executes a block of code as long as a specified condition remains true. It is often used when the number of iterations is unknown or depends on external factors, such as sensor values or user input.

Why is Important?

The *while* loop is important because it allows your program to keep running a block of code until a condition changes, making it useful in situations where the stopping point is uncertain. It is ideal for tasks that rely on real-time conditions, like waiting for a sensor to reach a certain threshold or monitoring a button press.

Syntax

```
while (condition) {
// code to execute
}
```

Syntax Explanation

- *while* starts the loop and checks the condition.
- *(condition)* is a logical expression that is evaluated before each iteration. If it is true, the code inside the loop runs; if false, the loop stops.
- The code inside the curly brackets *{}* runs repeatedly as long as the condition remains true.

Code Example

```
int sensorValue = analogRead(A0);
while (sensorValue < 500) {
sensorValue = analogRead(A0);
Serial.println("Waiting for sensor value to reach threshold...");
}
```

Notes

- A *while* loop is ideal for cases where you don't know in advance how many times the loop will run, such as waiting for a sensor reading or user action.
- Make sure the condition is updated within the loop, or it may result in an infinite loop.

Warnings

- Be cautious of infinite loops, where the condition never becomes false, which can cause your program to get stuck and unresponsive.
- Ensure that the condition in the *while* loop is checked and updated properly within the loop to avoid hanging the program.

Do-While Loop (do-while):

A *do-while* loop in Arduino is a variation of the *while* loop. The key difference is that in a *do-while* loop, the block of code runs at least once before the condition is checked. After the first execution, the loop continues as long as the specified condition is true.

Why is Important?

The *do-while* loop is important in scenarios where you need to ensure that a block of code runs at least once, regardless of the condition. This is useful when the code needs to execute and gather data before evaluating the condition, such as in cases where input or sensor readings are required for decision-making.

Syntax

```
do {
// code to execute
} while (condition);
```

Syntax Explanation

- *do* starts the loop by executing the code block at least once.
- The code inside the curly brackets *{}* is executed first.
- *while* checks the condition after the first iteration. If the condition is true, the loop continues; if false, the loop stops.

Code Example

```
int counter = 0;
do {
Serial.println(counter);
counter++;
} while (counter < 5);
```

Notes

- The main difference between *do-while* and *while* loops is that *do-while* guarantees at least one execution of the code block, even if the condition is false initially.
- The *do-while* loop can be useful for tasks that must be executed at least once, like initializing hardware or prompting for input.

Warnings

- Like the *while* loop, be cautious of infinite loops. Ensure that the condition will eventually become false, or the program may get stuck.
- Remember that the condition is checked after the loop's first run, so the code inside the loop may execute even when the condition is false.

3. Branching Statements

Break Statement (break):

A *break* statement in Arduino is used to exit a loop (such as *for*, *while*, or *do-while*) or a *switch* statement before it has completed all its iterations. When a *break* statement is encountered, the program jumps out of the loop or switch and continues with the next part of the code.

Why is Important?
The *break* statement is important because it allows you to stop a loop or switch statement early based on specific conditions. This can help optimize your code, improve performance, and allow for greater control over when certain operations should end, like exiting a loop once a desired result is achieved.

Syntax

```
break;
```

Syntax Explanation

- *break* is a standalone statement that is used inside a loop or switch.
- When *break* is encountered, it immediately terminates the loop or switch statement and moves the program execution to the next line after the loop or switch.

Code Example

```
for (int i = 0; i < 10; i++) {
if (i == 5) {
break;
}
Serial.println(i);
}
```

Notes

- The *break* statement is commonly used in *for*, *while*, and *do-while* loops when you want to exit the loop based on a certain condition.
- It is also used in *switch* statements to prevent the program from executing all the cases once a matching case is found.

Warnings

- Be cautious when using *break* in loops, as it can make the loop exit unexpectedly, which may lead to incomplete processing of data.
- Using *break* in nested loops will only exit the innermost loop. If you need to break out of multiple loops, you will need additional logic to handle that.

Continue Statement (continue):

A *continue* statement in Arduino is used within loops to skip the remaining code in the current iteration and move directly to the next iteration of the loop. It allows you to bypass certain parts of the loop's code under specific conditions without stopping the entire loop.

Why is Important?

The *continue* statement is important because it gives you more control over the flow of loops. It is especially useful when you want to ignore certain values or conditions and move on to the next iteration, making your code more efficient and concise. For example,

you can use *continue* to skip processing specific data points that
don't meet a condition.

Syntax

```
continue;
```

Syntax Explanation

- *continue* is a standalone statement that skips the rest of the
  code inside the current loop iteration.
- The loop then moves to the next iteration without executing
  the remaining code in the current one.

Code Example

```
for (int i = 0; i < 10; i++) {
if (i % 2 == 0) {
continue;
}
Serial.println(i);
}
```

Notes

- The *continue* statement is useful for skipping certain
  iterations in *for*, *while*, and *do-while* loops when a specific
  condition is met.
- It does not terminate the loop; it simply skips the current
  iteration and proceeds with the next one.

Warnings

- Be careful when using *continue* in loops with complex logic,
  as it may cause some parts of the loop to be skipped
  unintentionally, leading to bugs or unexpected behavior.

- Like the *break* statement, *continue* only affects the loop it is placed in and does not affect outer loops in nested loop scenarios.

4. Switch Case Statement
Switch Statement (switch):

A *switch* statement in Arduino is a control structure that allows you to choose and execute a specific block of code based on the value of a variable. It's an efficient alternative to using multiple *if-else if* conditions when you have many possible outcomes for a variable.

Why is Important?
The *switch* statement is important because it simplifies the code when you need to execute different actions based on a variable's value. Instead of writing multiple *if-else if* statements, you can use *switch* to clearly manage different cases. This makes the code cleaner and easier to maintain when dealing with multiple possibilities.

Syntax

```
switch (variable) {
case value1:
// code to execute if variable == value1
break;
case value2:
// code to execute if variable == value2
break;
...
default:
// code to execute if none of the cases are true
}
```

Syntax Explanation

- *switch (variable)*: The *switch* statement checks the value of *variable*.
- *case value1:*: If *variable* matches *value1*, the code block for this case is executed.

- *break;:* The *break* statement ends the case and prevents the execution from continuing to the next case.
- *default::* Optional. This block runs if none of the other cases match the variable's value.

Code Example

```
int mode = 2;
switch (mode) {
case 1:
Serial.println("Mode 1 selected");
break;
case 2:
Serial.println("Mode 2 selected");
break;
default:
Serial.println("Unknown mode");
}
```

Notes

- The *default* case is optional, but it's good practice to include it to handle unexpected values.
- Each case block should end with a *break* statement to prevent the program from executing the next case in the sequence unintentionally.

Warnings

- Forgetting the *break* statement can result in "fall-through" behavior, where multiple cases are executed in sequence, which may lead to unexpected behavior.
- The *switch* statement only works with integer-like data types (e.g., *int*, *char*) in Arduino. You cannot use it with floating-point numbers or strings.

5. Error Handling

Try-Catch (ESP-IDF):

The *try-catch* statement is a control structure used for error handling in the ESP-IDF environment. It allows the program to attempt to execute a block of code (*try* block) and, if an error occurs, handle that error in a separate block of code (*catch* block). While this feature is not available in Arduino, it is supported in the more advanced ESP-IDF (Espressif IoT Development Framework) for ESP32 development.

Why is Important?

The *try-catch* statement is important in complex applications where errors can occur during execution (e.g., file handling, network communication, or hardware failures). Instead of allowing the program to crash or behave unpredictably, *try-catch* enables developers to manage errors gracefully, by catching exceptions and taking corrective actions, such as retrying operations or logging errors.

Syntax

```
try {
// code to try
} catch (exception) {
// code to handle the error
}
```

Syntax Explanation

- *try*: Defines the block of code where errors may occur.
- *catch*: Defines a block of code that will handle any exceptions or errors that occur in the *try* block.
- *(exception)*: Optionally captures information about the error that occurred.

Code Example

```
try {
// Attempt to read a file
readFile("/data.txt");
} catch (FileNotFoundException e) {
// Handle the file not found error
Serial.println("File not found!");
}
```

Notes

- The *try-catch* statement is available only in the ESP-IDF environment, which provides lower-level access to hardware and more control over error handling than standard Arduino libraries.
- This feature is particularly useful in larger, more complex projects where you want to avoid program crashes due to unexpected runtime errors.

Warnings

- The *try-catch* mechanism adds overhead to your program, so use it judiciously, especially in performance-critical sections.
- Not all errors can be caught with *try-catch*. For example, hardware malfunctions or system-level failures may not be manageable with this mechanism.

Project-1.Simple Counter with Integer and For Loop for Arduino ESP32/ESP8266

Object:
Use an *int* variable to create a simple counter. In a *for* loop, increment the value of the counter from 0 to a set limit (e.g., 10) and display the counter value in the Serial Monitor at each iteration.

Requirement:

- ESP32 or ESP8266 board
- Arduino IDE

Circuit Connection:
No physical circuit is required. The Serial Monitor will be used to display the counter values.

Circuit Analysis:
The code will use an *int* variable to store the counter value. A *for* loop will be employed to increment this counter, and the updated value will be printed to the Serial Monitor during each iteration.

How it works:

1. An *int* variable is used to store the counter value.
2. A *for* loop increments the counter from 0 to a set limit (e.g., 10).
3. The Serial Monitor will display the counter value at each iteration.

Code:

```
void setup() {
    Serial.begin(115200);
    for (int counter = 0; counter <= 10; counter++) {
        Serial.print("Counter value: ");
        Serial.println(counter);
        delay(1000);
    }
}
void loop() {
}
```

Code Walkthrough:

- *Serial.begin(115200);* starts serial communication with the Serial Monitor.
- The *for* loop iterates from 0 to 10, incrementing the *int* variable *counter* with each iteration.
- *Serial.print()* and *Serial.println()* display the current counter value on the Serial Monitor during each loop iteration.
- The *delay(1000);* introduces a 1-second pause between iterations, making it easier to see each counter value.

Note:
This simple project demonstrates how to use an *int* variable and a *for* loop in Arduino programming. It helps beginners understand how loops work to increment values and display them using the Serial Monitor.

Project-2 Message Character Printer with Char Array and While Loop for Arduino ESP32/ESP8266

Store a message in a *char[]* array. Use a *while* loop to iterate through each character in the array and display them one by one on the Serial Monitor.

Requirement:

- ESP32 or ESP8266 board
- Arduino IDE

Circuit Connection:
No physical circuit is required. The Serial Monitor will be used to display each character of the message.

Circuit Analysis:
The code will use a *char[]* array to store the message. A *while* loop will iterate through each character in the array and display it on the Serial Monitor.

How it works:

1. A message is stored in a *char[]* array.
2. A *while* loop iterates through each character in the array.
3. The Serial Monitor displays each character one by one.

Code:

```
char message[] = "Hello, ESP32/ESP8266!";
int i = 0;
void setup() {
Serial.begin(115200);
while (message[i] != '\0') {
Serial.print(message[i]);
i++;
delay(500);
}
}
void loop() {}
```

Code Walkthrough:

- *char message[] = "Hello, ESP32/ESP8266!";* stores the message as an array of characters.
- *int index = 0;* initializes a variable to track the current character in the array.

- The *while* loop continues until the null terminator ('\0') at the end of the string is reached.
- *Serial.print(message[index]);* prints each character to the Serial Monitor one by one.
- *index++* moves to the next character in the array, and *delay(500);* introduces a 500ms delay between each character for readability.

Note:

This project demonstrates how to handle strings using a *char[]* array and a *while* loop. Each character in the array is printed to the Serial Monitor, providing beginners with a clear understanding of array iteration and character manipulation.

Project-3.Counter with Increment/Decrement and Conditional for Arduino ESP32/ESP8266

Use an *int* variable as a counter in a *for* loop. Use the modulus operator (%) to check if the counter is even or odd. If the counter is divisible by 2, display "Even" in the Serial Monitor; otherwise, display "Odd". The counter will be incremented using the (++) operator.

Requirement:

- ESP32 or ESP8266 board
- Arduino IDE

Circuit Analysis:

The code uses an *int* variable to store the counter value. A *for* loop controls the iteration, and the modulus operator (%) checks whether the number is even or odd. The *if* condition displays the appropriate message in the Serial Monitor.

How it works:

1. An *int* variable stores the counter value.
2. A *for* loop increments the counter from 0 to a defined limit.
3. The modulus operator (%) is used inside an *if* condition to determine if the counter is even or odd.

4. The Serial Monitor will display "Even" if the number is divisible by 2, otherwise "Odd".

Code:

```
void setup() {
    Serial.begin(115200);
    for (int counter = 0; counter <= 10; counter++) {
        if (counter % 2 == 0) {
            Serial.print(counter);
            Serial.println(" - Even");
        } else {
            Serial.print(counter);
            Serial.println(" - Odd");
        }
        delay(500);
    }
}
void loop() {
}
```

Code Walkthrough:

- *for (int counter = 0; counter <= 10; counter++)* loops from 0 to 10, incrementing *counter* by 1 in each iteration.
- Inside the *if* condition, *counter % 2 == 0* checks if the counter is divisible by 2 (i.e., an even number). If true, "Even" is displayed; otherwise, "Odd" is displayed.
- *Serial.print(counter);* prints the current value of the counter, followed by " - Even" or " - Odd" depending on the result of the modulus check.
- *delay(500);* adds a 500ms pause between each iteration for readability.

Note:
This project demonstrates the use of conditional checks with the modulus operator (%) to determine whether a number is even or odd. It also uses a *for* loop for iteration and the ++ operator to increment the counter.

Project-4. String Concatenation with Char Array and While Loop for Arduino ESP32/ESP8266

Store a message in a *char[]* array and concatenate its characters into a *String* using the + operator. Use a *while* loop to iterate through each character, form a complete word, and display it in the Serial Monitor.

Requirement:

- ESP32 or ESP8266 board
- Arduino IDE

Circuit Connection:
No physical circuit is required. The Serial Monitor will display the concatenated message.

Circuit Analysis:
The code will use a *char[]* array to store individual characters. A *while* loop will iterate through the array, and each character will be concatenated into a *String*. The final word will be displayed in the Serial Monitor.

How it works:

1. A *char[]* array is used to store individual characters of a message.
2. A *String* variable is used to concatenate the characters.
3. A *while* loop goes through each character in the *char[]* array and adds it to the *String* using the + operator.
4. The Serial Monitor will display the concatenated word after each loop.

Code:

```
char message[] = "ESP32";
String completeMessage = "";
int i = 0; // Renamed from index to i
void setup() {
Serial.begin(115200);
while (message[i] != '\0') {
completeMessage += message[i];
Serial.println(completeMessage);
i++; // Use i instead of index
delay(500);
```

```
}
}
void loop() {}
```

Code Walkthrough:

- *char message[] = "ESP32";* stores the message as individual characters in a *char[]* array.
- *String completeMessage = "";* initializes an empty *String* to concatenate the characters.
- The *while* loop continues until the null terminator ('\0') is reached, meaning the end of the *char[]* array.
- *completeMessage += message[index];* concatenates each character from the *char[]* array into the *String*.
- *Serial.println(completeMessage);* displays the progressively concatenated message in the Serial Monitor.
- *delay(500);* introduces a 500ms pause to make it easier to see the concatenation process.

Note:
This project demonstrates how to concatenate characters from a *char[]* array into a *String* using the + operator in Arduino. It's an excellent example for beginners to understand both character arrays and string manipulation using loops.

Chapter Summary

In this chapter, we covered the essential control structures used to manage the flow of Arduino programs on ESP32/ESP8266:

- **Conditional Statements**:
  - **If Statement (if)**: Used to execute a block of code when a condition is true.
  - **If-Else Statement (if-else)**: Allows the program to choose between two actions based on a condition being true or false.
  - **Else-If Ladder (if-else if)**: Evaluates multiple conditions in sequence, executing the code for the first true condition.
- **Looping Structures**:

- **For Loop (for)**: Repeats a block of code a specific number of times. Ideal when the number of iterations is known.
- **While Loop (while)**: Runs a block of code as long as a condition remains true. Used when the stopping point is unknown initially.
- **Do-While Loop (do-while)**: Similar to while, but guarantees that the code runs at least once before checking the condition.
- **Branching Statements**:
  - **Break Statement (break)**: Exits a loop or switch statement before it completes all iterations.
  - **Continue Statement (continue)**: Skips the rest of the current loop iteration and moves to the next iteration.
- **Switch Statement**:
  - **Switch Statement (switch)**: Efficiently handles multiple possible values for a variable, allowing specific code blocks to execute for each case.
- **Error Handling (ESP-IDF)**:
  - **Try-Catch Statement**: Available in ESP-IDF, useful for handling errors such as file not found or network failures. It prevents the program from crashing by catching exceptions.

These control structures are the backbone of decision-making and repetition in Arduino programming, enabling the microcontroller to respond dynamically to different conditions, execute tasks multiple times, and handle errors gracefully. Understanding how and when to use each of these control structures will help you create efficient, responsive, and reliable programs for ESP32 and ESP8266-based projects.

Chapter-4 Operators

In this chapter, we explore the different types of operators available in Arduino programming for ESP32 and ESP8266 microcontrollers. Operators are fundamental to performing calculations, making comparisons, and controlling program flow. We cover **Arithmetic Operators** for basic math operations, **Comparison Operators** for evaluating relationships between values, **Logical Operators** for combining multiple conditions, **Assignment Operators** for assigning and updating variable values, and **Bitwise Operators** for working with individual bits of data.

Syntax Table

Topics	Syntax	Simple Example
Addition (+)	result = value1 + value2;	int sum = a + b;
Subtraction (-)	result = value1 - value2;	int difference = a - b;
Multiplication (*)	result = value1 * value2;	int product = a * b;
Division (/)	result = value1 / value2;	int quotient = a / b;
Modulo (%)	result = value1 % value2;	int remainder = a % b;
Equal To (==)	value1 == value2;	if (a == b) { Serial.println("Equal") ; }

Not Equal To (!=)	value1 != value2;	if (a != b) { Serial.println("Not Equal"); }
Greater Than (>)	value1 > value2;	if (a > b) { Serial.println("Greater"); }
Less Than (<)	value1 < value2;	if (a < b) { Serial.println("Less"); }
Greater Than or Equal To (>=)	value1 >= value2;	if (a >= b) { Serial.println("Greater or Equal"); }
Less Than or Equal To (<=)	value1 <= value2;	if (a <= b) { Serial.println("Less or Equal"); }
Logical AND (&&)	condition1 && condition2;	if (a > 0 && b < 10) { Serial.println("Both True"); }
Logical OR (		)
Logical NOT (!)	!condition;	if (!a) { Serial.println("Not True"); }
Assignment (=)	variable = value;	int x = 10;
Addition Assignment (+=)	variable += value;	x += 5;

Subtraction Assignment (-=)	*variable -= value;*	*x -= 3;*
Multiplication Assignment (*=)	*variable = value;*	*x = 2;*
Division Assignment (/=)	*variable /= value;*	*x /= 4;*
Bitwise AND (&)	*result = value1 & value2;*	*int result = value1 & value2;*
Bitwise OR (	)		*result = value1*
Bitwise XOR (^)	*result = value1 ^ value2;*	*int result = value1 ^ value2;*
Bitwise NOT (~)	*result = ~value;*	*int result = ~value;*

1. Arithmetic Operators

Addition (+):

The addition operator + is an arithmetic operator that adds two numbers. In Arduino, this operator can be used with both integer and floating-point numbers, allowing you to sum values like sensor readings, counters, or variables.

Why is Important?

The addition operator is essential for performing basic math operations, which are the building blocks of many algorithms. Whether you need to sum sensor values, add to a counter, or calculate a total, the + operator provides a simple and effective way to do so in your code.

Syntax

```
result = value1 + value2;
```

Syntax Explanation

- *result* is where the sum of *value1* and *value2* is stored.
- *value1* and *value2* are the two numbers or variables being added together.

Code Example

```
int a = 7;
int b = 3;
int sum = a + b;
Serial.println(sum); // Output: 10
```

Notes

- The addition operator can work with integers and floating-point numbers. If either operand is a floating-point number, the result will be a floating-point value.

Warnings

- Be cautious of variable overflow, especially when adding large numbers that might exceed the range of the variable's data type. For example, adding two large integers that exceed the maximum value of an *int* can cause unexpected results.
- Ensure that you're using the appropriate data type when working with floating-point numbers to avoid losing precision.

Subtraction (-):

The subtraction operator - is an arithmetic operator in Arduino that subtracts one number from another. It can be used with integers, floating-point numbers, or variables to calculate the difference between two values.

Why is Important?

The - operator is essential for performing mathematical operations that require finding the difference between values. This is useful for applications like measuring changes in sensor values, calculating offsets, or performing real-time computations where subtraction is necessary.

Syntax

```
result = value1 - value2;
```

Syntax Explanation

- *result* is the variable that will store the difference.
- *value1* and *value2* are the numbers or variables, with *value2* being subtracted from *value1*.

Code Example

```
int a = 10;
int b = 4;
int difference = a - b;
Serial.println(difference); // Output: 6
```

Notes

- The subtraction operator works with both integers and floating-point numbers. If either operand is a floating-point number, the result will also be a floating-point number.

Warnings

- Be mindful of data types when subtracting, as underflow can occur if the result is smaller than the minimum value that the data type can store (e.g., subtracting a large number from a small number when using unsigned integers).
- Ensure proper use of floating-point data types when precision is required to avoid truncation of decimal values.

Multiplication (*):

The multiplication operator * in Arduino multiplies two numbers together. It can be used with both integers and floating-point numbers to compute the product of two values.

Why is Important?
The multiplication operator is essential in many calculations, such as scaling sensor readings, converting units, or computing areas and volumes. It allows for more complex mathematical operations that go beyond simple addition or subtraction, making it crucial in real-time applications.

Syntax

```
result = value1 * value2;
```

Syntax Explanation

- *result* stores the product of the two numbers or variables.
- *value1* and *value2* are the numbers or variables to be multiplied.

Code Example

```
int a = 5;
int b = 6;
int product = a * b;
Serial.println(product); // Output: 30
```

Notes

- Multiplication works with both integers and floating-point numbers. If either operand is a floating-point number, the result will be a floating-point value.

Warnings

- Be mindful of variable overflow when multiplying large numbers, especially with smaller data types like *int*. The result may exceed the maximum value the data type can hold, leading to incorrect results.
- Ensure that you are using the correct data types, especially when precision is required in floating-point calculations, to avoid rounding errors.

Division (/):

The division operator / is used in Arduino to divide one number by another. It works with both whole numbers (integers) and decimal numbers (floating-point) to calculate the result.

Why is Important?
Division is important for tasks like calculating averages, scaling values, or converting units. It helps split a number into smaller parts, which is crucial in many real-time applications like sensor data processing or calculating ratios.

Syntax

```
result = value1 / value2;
```

Syntax Explanation

- *result* is where the result of the division will be stored.
- *value1* is the number to be divided (dividend).
- *value2* is the number you're dividing by (divisor).

Code Example

```
int a = 20;
int b = 4;
int quotient = a / b;
Serial.println(quotient); // Output: 5
```

Notes

- When dividing two whole numbers (integers), the result will be a whole number, and any decimals will be discarded. For example, *7 / 2* results in *3*, not *3.5*.
- To get a result with decimal places, use at least one decimal number (like *float* or *double*) in the division.

Warnings

- Be careful not to divide by zero, as this will cause errors. Always check that the divisor (*value2*) is not zero.
- Integer division may give you an unexpected result if you need decimal values, so use floating-point numbers for more precision when necessary.

Modulo (%):

The modulo operator % in Arduino returns the remainder after dividing one number by another. It is used with whole numbers (integers) and is helpful when you need to determine what remains after dividing numbers.

Why is Important?
The modulo operator is useful in situations where you need to check if a number is divisible by another, or when you need to loop back or cycle through values (e.g., when working with timers, counters, or arrays). It's commonly used to detect even/odd numbers or create repeating patterns.

Syntax

```
result = value1 % value2;
```

Syntax Explanation

- *result* stores the remainder of the division of *value1* by *value2*.
- *value1* is the dividend (number to be divided).

- *value2* is the divisor (the number you're dividing by).

Code Example

```
int a = 10;
int b = 3;
int remainder = a % b;
Serial.println(remainder); // Output: 1 (because 10 / 3 gives a
remainder of 1)
```

Notes

- The modulo operator only works with integers. It gives you the remainder from dividing two numbers, which can be helpful for determining factors or checking if a number is divisible by another.

Warnings

- Do not use modulo with zero as the divisor (*value2*). Dividing by zero causes an error.
- Modulo only works with whole numbers. If you need to handle decimals, you'll need a different approach, as % does not work with floating-point numbers.

2. Comparison Operators

Equal To (==):

The == operator in Arduino checks if two values are equal. It is a comparison operator that evaluates whether the value on the left side is the same as the value on the right side, returning either *true* or *false*.

Why is Important?
The == operator is essential for making decisions in your code. It is commonly used in conditions like *if* statements to compare values, such as checking sensor readings, comparing user input, or controlling the flow of your program based on specific values.

Syntax

```
value1 == value2;
```

Syntax Explanation

- *value1* and *value2* are the values or variables being compared.
- If *value1* is equal to *value2*, the expression returns *true*; otherwise, it returns *false*.

Code Example

```
int a = 5;
int b = 5;
if (a == b) {
Serial.println("a is equal to b");
}
```

Notes

- The == operator compares values and returns a Boolean result (*true* or *false*), which is useful for decision-making in control structures like *if*, *while*, and *for* loops.
- Be careful not to confuse the == operator (equality check) with the = operator (assignment).

Warnings

- Using = instead of == in comparisons is a common mistake. = assigns a value, while == checks equality. This error can lead to bugs that are difficult to debug.
- The == operator works for comparing both integers and floating-point numbers, but due to the precision limits of floating-point numbers, comparing two floats may not always work as expected. Use caution when comparing floating-point values directly.

Not Equal To (!=):

The *!=* operator in Arduino is a comparison operator that checks if two values are not equal. If the values are different, the expression returns *true*. If the values are the same, it returns *false*.

Why is Important?
The *!=* operator is important for decision-making in your code when you need to execute certain actions if two values are not the same. It helps control program flow by checking conditions like when a sensor value does not match a target, or when user input is incorrect.

Syntax

```
value1 != value2;
```

Syntax Explanation

- *value1* and *value2* are the values or variables being compared.
- If *value1* is not equal to *value2*, the expression evaluates to *true*. Otherwise, it evaluates to *false*.

Code Example

```
int a = 5;
int b = 3;
if (a != b) {
Serial.println("a is not equal to b");
}
```

Notes

- The *!=* operator is the inverse of the == operator. It is often used in loops and conditions to check if something is not equal to a specific value, enabling flexibility in controlling the flow of your program.

Warnings

- As with the == operator, be cautious when using != with floating-point numbers due to precision limitations. Direct comparisons between floating-point numbers may not behave as expected because of rounding errors.
- Ensure that you're using != properly for comparisons, and don't confuse it with other operators, as that could lead to logical errors in your program.

Greater Than (>):

The > operator in Arduino is a comparison operator that checks if one value is greater than another. If the value on the left is larger than the value on the right, the expression returns *true*. If not, it returns *false*.

Why is Important?
The > operator is crucial for making decisions based on size or value. It is often used in control structures to execute code when one value exceeds another, such as checking if a sensor reading is above a threshold or determining if a timer has passed a certain limit.

Syntax

```
value1 > value2;
```

Syntax Explanation

- *value1* and *value2* are the two values or variables being compared.
- The expression evaluates to *true* if *value1* is greater than *value2*, otherwise it evaluates to *false*.

Code Example

```
int temperature = 25;
if (temperature > 20) {
Serial.println("It's warm enough!");
}
```

Notes

- The > operator works with both integers and floating-point numbers. It is commonly used in conditional statements like *if*, *while*, and *for* loops.

Warnings

- Be careful when comparing floating-point numbers, as precision limitations can lead to unexpected results when using the > operator.
- Make sure both values being compared are of compatible types to avoid errors or unintended behavior in your program.

Less Than (<):

The < operator in Arduino is a comparison operator that checks if one value is less than another. If the value on the left is smaller than the value on the right, the expression returns *true*. Otherwise, it returns *false*.

Why is Important?

The < operator is essential for decision-making when you need to check if one value is smaller than another. It is commonly used in control structures to trigger actions when a value falls below a threshold, such as ensuring that a temperature, sensor value, or timer hasn't exceeded a limit.

Syntax

```
value1 < value2;
```

Syntax Explanation

- *value1* and *value2* are the values or variables being compared.
- The expression evaluates to *true* if *value1* is less than *value2*; otherwise, it evaluates to *false*.

Code Example

```
int temperature = 15;
if (temperature < 20) {
Serial.println("It's too cold!");
}
```

Notes

- The < operator works with both integers and floating-point numbers. It's often used in conditional statements like *if*, *while*, and *for* loops to manage program flow based on numeric conditions.

Warnings

- Be cautious when comparing floating-point numbers due to possible precision errors.
- Ensure that both values being compared are of the correct data types to avoid unexpected results or errors in your program.

Greater Than or Equal To (>=):

The >= operator in Arduino checks if one value is greater than or equal to another. It compares two values and returns *true* if the value on the left is greater than or equal to the value on the right. If not, it returns *false*.

Why is Important?

The >= operator is important for situations where you need to check if a value has reached or surpassed a certain threshold. It is useful in controlling program flow, such as ensuring that a condition is met before proceeding, or monitoring values like sensor readings, timers, or counters.

Syntax

```
value1 >= value2;
```

Syntax Explanation

- *value1* and *value2* are the values being compared.
- The expression evaluates to *true* if *value1* is greater than or equal to *value2*, otherwise it evaluates to *false*.

Code Example

```
int score = 85;
if (score >= 60) {
Serial.println("You passed the exam!");
}
```

Notes

- The >= operator works with both integers and floating-point numbers. It is often used in control structures like *if*, *while*, or *for* loops.

Warnings

- Be cautious when comparing floating-point numbers due to potential precision errors.
- Ensure both values are of compatible data types to avoid issues or unexpected behavior.

Less Than or Equal To (<=):

The <= operator in Arduino checks if one value is less than or equal to another. It compares two values and returns *true* if the value on the left is less than or equal to the value on the right. If not, it returns *false*.

Why is Important?

The <= operator is essential for situations where you need to check if a value has fallen below or reached a certain threshold. It is commonly used in control structures to manage program flow, such as ensuring values don't exceed a limit or triggering actions when a specific condition is met.

Syntax

```
value1 <= value2;
```

Syntax Explanation

- *value1* and *value2* are the values being compared.
- The expression evaluates to *true* if *value1* is less than or equal to *value2*, otherwise it evaluates to *false*.

Code Example

```
int temperature = 18;
if (temperature <= 20) {
Serial.println("Temperature is below or equal to 20 degrees.");
}
```

Notes

- The <= operator works with both integers and floating-point numbers. It is commonly used in conditional statements like *if*, *while*, or *for* loops.

Warnings

- Be cautious when comparing floating-point numbers, as precision limitations might cause unexpected results.
- Ensure both values are of compatible data types to avoid errors or incorrect behavior.

3. Logical Operators

Logical AND (&&):

The && operator in Arduino is a logical operator that returns *true* only if both conditions being compared are true. If either one of the conditions is false, the entire expression evaluates to *false*.

Why is Important?

The && operator is important for decision-making when multiple conditions must be met simultaneously. It allows for more complex logic in control structures, such as ensuring that multiple variables meet certain criteria before executing a specific block of code. It's often used when checking multiple sensor values, input states, or conditions together.

Syntax

```
condition1 && condition2;
```

Syntax Explanation

- *condition1* and *condition2* are the two logical expressions being evaluated.
- The expression returns *true* if both conditions are true, otherwise it returns *false*.

Code Example

```
int temp = 25;
int humidity = 60;
if (temp > 20 && humidity < 70) {
Serial.println("Conditions are ideal!");
}
```

Notes

- The && operator is useful for combining multiple conditions in *if*, *while*, and *for* loops, allowing for more precise control of program flow.

- Both conditions must be true for the entire expression to evaluate as true.

Warnings

- Make sure the conditions in the expression are correctly evaluated to avoid unexpected results.
- Using complex expressions with multiple logical operators can make the code harder to read and debug, so ensure clarity when using &&.

Logical OR (||):

The || operator in Arduino is a logical operator that returns *true* if at least one of the conditions being evaluated is true. It returns *false* only if both conditions are false.

Why is Important?
The || operator is important for scenarios where you want to execute a block of code if at least one of multiple conditions is met. It allows for flexible decision-making in control structures, like checking if either of two input signals are active or if one of several conditions is true.

Syntax

```
condition1 || condition2;
```

Syntax Explanation

- *condition1* and *condition2* are the two logical expressions being evaluated.
- The expression returns *true* if at least one condition is true, and *false* only if both conditions are false.

Code Example

```
int button1 = digitalRead(2);
int button2 = digitalRead(3);
```

```
if (button1 == HIGH || button2 == HIGH) {
Serial.println("At least one button is pressed.");
}
```

Notes

- The || operator is often used in *if*, *while*, or *for* loops where you need to check if one of several conditions is true, allowing more flexibility in decision-making.
- The expression will evaluate to *true* as long as at least one condition is true.

Warnings

- Be cautious when using || with complex conditions, as it may become harder to understand and debug.
- Ensure both conditions are evaluated properly to avoid logic errors in your program.

Logical NOT (!):

The *!* operator in Arduino is a logical operator that inverts the result of a condition. If the condition is *true*, the *!* operator returns *false*. If the condition is *false*, it returns *true*.

Why is Important?

The *!* operator is useful for situations where you need to check if a condition is *not* true. It allows you to reverse the logic of a condition, which is essential in control structures like *if* statements to perform actions when something is false instead of true. For example, checking if a button is not pressed or if a sensor value is not within a certain range.

Syntax

```
!condition;
```

Syntax Explanation

- *condition* is the logical expression being evaluated.
- The *!* operator inverts the result of the condition, returning *true* if the condition is *false*, and *false* if the condition is *true*.

Code Example

```
int buttonState = digitalRead(2);
if (!buttonState) {
Serial.println("Button is not pressed.");
}
```

Notes

- The *!* operator is typically used in situations where you want to check the opposite of a condition, making it useful in *if*, *while*, and *for* loops.

Warnings

- Be mindful of readability when using *!* in complex expressions, as it can sometimes make the logic harder to follow.
- Ensure the condition is evaluated correctly, as misunderstanding the logic could lead to incorrect behavior in your program.

4. Assignment Operators

Assignment (=):

The assignment operator = in Arduino assigns a value to a variable. It is used to store a specific value in a variable for later use in the program. This operator updates the value of the variable on the left side with the value on the right side.

Why is Important?

The assignment operator is fundamental for storing data in variables, which is essential for any program. Without the ability to assign values, it would be impossible to keep track of or update the state of variables, sensor readings, or calculations during a program's execution.

Syntax

```
variable = value;
```

Syntax Explanation

- *variable* is the name of the variable where the value will be stored.
- *value* is the number, character, or expression assigned to the variable.

Code Example

```
int sensorValue = 0;
sensorValue = analogRead(A0);
Serial.println(sensorValue);
```

Notes

- The assignment operator sets the value of a variable, which can be an initial value or a calculated one.
- Be careful not to confuse the assignment operator = with the equality operator ==, which checks if two values are equal.

Warnings

- Using = in place of == in conditional expressions (like *if* statements) can cause logical errors, as = assigns a value rather than checking equality.

- Ensure the data type of the variable is appropriate for the value being assigned to avoid unexpected behavior or data loss.

Addition Assignment (+=):

The addition assignment operator += in Arduino adds a value to a variable and then assigns the result back to that same variable. It is a shorthand way of writing a longer addition and assignment statement.

Why is Important?
The += operator is important because it simplifies the process of updating a variable's value, especially in loops or cumulative calculations. It makes the code more concise and readable when adding a value to a variable repeatedly, such as in counters, timers, or running totals.

Syntax

```
variable += value;
```

Syntax Explanation

- *variable* is the variable that will have *value* added to it.
- *value* is the number or expression being added to *variable*. The result is then stored back in *variable*.

Code Example

```
int counter = 0;
counter += 5; // counter is now 5
counter += 3; // counter is now 8
Serial.println(counter); // Output: 8
```

Notes

- The += operator is a convenient way to add and assign in one step. It is frequently used in loops to increment values or track totals over time.
- The operator works with both integers and floating-point numbers.

Warnings

- Be mindful of overflow when using the += operator with integers, especially when adding large values. If the result exceeds the range of the variable's data type, unexpected results may occur.
- Ensure that the data types of the variable and value are compatible to avoid truncation or data loss when using floating-point numbers.

Subtraction Assignment (-=):

The subtraction assignment operator -= in Arduino subtracts a value from a variable and then assigns the result back to that variable. It is a shorthand way of writing a subtraction and assignment statement in one step.

Why is Important?
The -= operator is useful when you need to decrease the value of a variable repeatedly, such as in countdowns, timers, or when tracking resources. It makes the code cleaner and easier to read by eliminating the need for a longer subtraction and assignment statement.

Syntax

```
variable -= value;
```

Syntax Explanation

- *variable* is the variable from which *value* will be subtracted.
- *value* is the number or expression being subtracted. The result is then stored back in *variable*.

Code Example

```
int count = 10;
count -= 3; // count is now 7
count -= 2; // count is now 5
Serial.println(count); // Output: 5
```

Notes

- The -= operator is commonly used in loops to decrease a value over time, such as in countdowns or to adjust values based on conditions.
- The operator works with both integers and floating-point numbers.

Warnings

- Be careful of underflow when using the -= operator, especially when subtracting large values from small numbers. If the result becomes negative and the variable is an unsigned data type, this could lead to unexpected results.
- Ensure that the data types of the variable and value are compatible to avoid data loss, particularly when using floating-point numbers.

Multiplication Assignment (*=):

The multiplication assignment operator *= in Arduino multiplies a variable by a value and then assigns the result back to that variable. It combines multiplication and assignment in one step.

Why is Important?

The *= operator simplifies the code when you need to repeatedly multiply a variable by a certain value, such as in scaling calculations, cumulative product computations, or exponential growth scenarios. It makes the code cleaner by eliminating the need for a longer multiplication and assignment statement.

Syntax

```
variable *= value;
```

Syntax Explanation

- *variable* is the variable being multiplied by *value*.
- *value* is the number or expression that *variable* is multiplied by. The result is then stored back in *variable*.

Code Example

```
int result = 5;
result *= 3; // result is now 15
result *= 2; // result is now 30
Serial.println(result); // Output: 30
```

Notes

- The *= operator is a convenient way to perform multiplication and assignment in one line, which is especially useful in loops or iterative calculations.
- It works with both integers and floating-point numbers.

Warnings

- Be cautious of overflow when using *= with integers. Multiplying large numbers may exceed the maximum value of the data type, leading to incorrect results.
- Ensure the data types of the variable and value are compatible, especially when using floating-point numbers, to avoid loss of precision or truncation.

Division Assignment (/=):

The division assignment operator /= in Arduino divides a variable by a value and then assigns the result back to that variable. It combines division and assignment into one step.

Why is Important?
The /= operator simplifies the code when you need to repeatedly

divide a variable by a certain value, such as in scaling down values, adjusting sensor readings, or performing iterative calculations. It makes the code more concise by eliminating the need for separate division and assignment operations.

Syntax

```
variable /= value;
```

Syntax Explanation

- *variable* is the variable being divided by *value*.
- *value* is the number or expression that *variable* is divided by. The result is then stored back in *variable*.

Code Example

```
int result = 100;
result /= 4; // result is now 25
result /= 5; // result is now 5
Serial.println(result); // Output: 5
```

Notes

- The /= operator is useful for performing division and assignment in a single line, making the code cleaner.
- It works with both integers and floating-point numbers.

Warnings

- Be careful when using /= with integers, as dividing by zero will result in an error. Always check that the divisor is not zero.
- When dividing integers, the result will be an integer (any remainder will be discarded). If you need more precise results, use floating-point numbers.

5. Bitwise Operators

Bitwise AND (&):

The & operator in Arduino performs a bitwise AND operation between two numbers. This operation compares each bit of two numbers, and if both corresponding bits are 1, the result will be 1; otherwise, it will be 0.

Why is Important?

The bitwise AND operator is important for low-level programming tasks, such as manipulating individual bits of data, performing masking operations, or checking specific flags in hardware registers. It is often used in embedded systems to control specific hardware features or read specific bits from sensors or registers.

Syntax

```
result = value1 & value2;
```

Syntax Explanation

- *value1* and *value2* are the two numbers whose bits will be compared.
- The result will contain 1 only in the bit positions where both *value1* and *value2* have 1; otherwise, the bit will be 0.

Code Example

```
int value1 = 6; // binary: 0110
int value2 = 3; // binary: 0011
int result = value1 & value2;
Serial.println(result); // Output: 2 (binary: 0010)
```

Notes

- The bitwise AND operator is often used to mask out specific bits from a number. For example, it can be used to isolate certain bits in a sensor reading or to manipulate hardware registers.

Warnings

- Be careful when using bitwise operators with signed integers, as the result can be unexpected due to how negative numbers are stored in memory (using two's complement).
- Always ensure you understand the bit-level operations before applying them to avoid incorrect results in critical applications.

Bitwise OR (|):

The | operator in Arduino performs a bitwise OR operation between two numbers. This operation compares each bit of two numbers, and if either of the corresponding bits is 1, the result will be 1; otherwise, it will be 0.

Why is Important?
The bitwise OR operator is important for setting specific bits in a number while preserving the other bits. It is commonly used in embedded systems for setting flags, manipulating hardware registers, and enabling specific bits without affecting others.

Syntax

```
result = value1 | value2;
```

Syntax Explanation

- *value1* and *value2* are the two numbers whose bits will be compared.
- The result will have a bit set to 1 if either *value1* or *value2* has a 1 in that position; otherwise, it will be 0.

Code Example

```
int value1 = 6; // binary: 0110
int value2 = 3; // binary: 0011
int result = value1 | value2;
Serial.println(result); // Output: 7 (binary: 0111)
```

Notes

- The bitwise OR operator is often used to combine flags or set specific bits in a value without changing the others. For example, it can be used to enable multiple options or settings by combining bits.

Warnings

- Be cautious when using bitwise operators with signed integers, as they may produce unexpected results due to how negative numbers are represented in memory (two's complement).
- Ensure you understand the bit-level effects of using the OR operator, especially when working with hardware registers or specific bit manipulations.

Bitwise XOR (^)

The Bitwise XOR (^) operator compares the bits of two numbers. If the bits in a certain position are different, the result will be 1. If the bits are the same, the result will be 0. This is useful for operations that need to toggle or flip bits.

Why is Important

The Bitwise XOR operator helps you toggle specific bits in a number. It is often used to flip the state of a bit without changing the others, which is important in controlling flags, states, or hardware registers. XOR is also key in encryption and checksum calculations.

Syntax

```
result = value1 ^ value2;
```

Syntax Explanation

value1 and *value2* are two numbers. The XOR operation checks their bits one by one. If the bits at a particular position are different, the result will have 1 in that position. If they are the same, the result will be 0.

Code Example

```
int value1 = 6; // binary: 0110
int value2 = 3; // binary: 0011
int result = value1 ^ value2;
Serial.println(result); // Output: 5 (binary: 0101)
```

Notes

- XOR is often used to toggle specific bits, making it useful in situations where you need to change specific settings or states without affecting other data.
- XOR of two identical bits is always 0, and XOR of two different bits is always 1.

Warnings

- Be careful when using XOR with negative numbers, as they are stored in a special format called two's complement, which can lead to unexpected results.
- It's important to fully understand XOR before using it, especially when dealing with hardware registers, as a mistake could cause unpredictable behavior in your system.

Bitwise NOT (~)

The Bitwise NOT (~) operator inverts all the bits in a number. This means that each 0 becomes a 1, and each 1 becomes a 0. It's commonly used to reverse bit patterns or prepare data for specific logical operations.

Why is Important
The Bitwise NOT operator is essential when you need to flip all bits in a number. It can be useful in many situations like changing polarity in hardware control or preparing data for bitmask operations. In embedded systems, manipulating bits is often necessary for low-

level hardware interactions, and NOT makes it easy to reverse states.

Syntax

```
result = ~value;
```

Syntax Explanation

value is the number whose bits will be inverted. The result will have 1s where *value* had 0s, and 0s where *value* had 1s.

Code Example

```
int value = 6; // binary: 00000110
int result = ~value;
Serial.println(result); // Output: -7 (binary: 11111001 in 2's
complement)
```

Notes

- The Bitwise NOT operation flips every bit, including the sign bit in signed numbers, which can lead to a negative result due to the two's complement representation of negative numbers.
- This operation is frequently used in creating bitmasks or preparing data for specific bit-level manipulations in hardware.

Warnings

- Be careful with signed numbers because flipping the bits will also affect the sign, potentially leading to unexpected negative values.
- Understand how the Bitwise NOT affects the entire 8, 16, or 32-bit number format to avoid unwanted results, especially when working with unsigned and signed numbers in embedded systems.

Project- 1.Counter with Increment/Decrement and Conditional for Arduino ESP32/ESP8266

Use an int variable as a counter in a for loop. Use the modulus operator (%) to check if the counter is even or odd. If the counter is divisible by 2, display "Even" in the Serial Monitor; otherwise, display "Odd". The counter will be incremented using the (++) operator.

Requirement:

- ESP32 or ESP8266 board
- Arduino IDE

Circuit Connection:

No physical circuit is required. The Serial Monitor will be used to display the counter's status (Even or Odd).

Circuit Analysis:

The code uses an *int* variable to store the counter value. A *for* loop controls the iteration, and the modulus operator (%) checks whether the number is even or odd. The *if* condition displays the appropriate message in the Serial Monitor.

How it works:

1. An *int* variable stores the counter value.
2. A *for* loop increments the counter from 0 to a defined limit.
3. The modulus operator (%) is used inside an *if* condition to determine if the counter is even or odd.
4. The Serial Monitor will display "Even" if the number is divisible by 2, otherwise "Odd".

Code:

```
void setup() {
    Serial.begin(115200);
    for (int counter = 0; counter <= 10; counter++) {
        if (counter % 2 == 0) {
            Serial.print(counter);
            Serial.println(" - Even");
        } else {
```

```
            Serial.print(counter);
            Serial.println(" - Odd");
        }
        delay(500);
    }
}
void loop() {
}
```

Code Walkthrough:

- *for (int counter = 0; counter <= 10; counter++)* loops from 0 to 10, incrementing *counter* by 1 in each iteration.
- Inside the *if* condition, *counter % 2 == 0* checks if the counter is divisible by 2 (i.e., an even number). If true, "Even" is displayed; otherwise, "Odd" is displayed.
- *Serial.print(counter);* prints the current value of the counter, followed by " - Even" or " - Odd" depending on the result of the modulus check.
- *delay(500);* adds a 500ms pause between each iteration for readability.

Note:
This project demonstrates the use of conditional checks with the modulus operator (%) to determine whether a number is even or odd. It also uses a *for* loop for iteration and the ++ operator to increment the counter.

2. String Concatenation with Char Array and While Loop for Arduino ESP32/ESP8266

Object:
Store a message in a *char[]* array and concatenate its characters into a *String* using the + operator. Use a *while* loop to iterate through each character, form a complete word, and display it in the Serial Monitor.

Requirement:

- ESP32 or ESP8266 board
- Arduino IDE

Circuit Connection:

No physical circuit is required. The Serial Monitor will display the concatenated message.

Circuit Analysis:

The code will use a *char[]* array to store individual characters. A *while* loop will iterate through the array, and each character will be concatenated into a *String*. The final word will be displayed in the Serial Monitor.

How it works:

1. A *char[]* array is used to store individual characters of a message.
2. A *String* variable is used to concatenate the characters.
3. A *while* loop goes through each character in the *char[]* array and adds it to the *String* using the + operator.
4. The Serial Monitor will display the concatenated word after each loop.

Code:

```
char message[] = "ESP32";
String completeMessage = "";
int i = 0; // Renamed from index to i
void setup() {
Serial.begin(115200);
while (message[i] != '\0') {
completeMessage += message[i];
Serial.println(completeMessage);
i++; // Use i instead of index
delay(500);
}
}
void loop() {}
```

Code Walkthrough:

- *char message[] = "ESP32";* stores the message as individual characters in a *char[]* array.

- *String completeMessage = "";* initializes an empty *String* to concatenate the characters.
- The *while* loop continues until the null terminator ('\0') is reached, meaning the end of the *char[]* array.
- *completeMessage += message[index];* concatenates each character from the *char[]* array into the *String*.
- *Serial.println(completeMessage);* displays the progressively concatenated message in the Serial Monitor.
- *delay(500);* introduces a 500ms pause to make it easier to see the concatenation process.

Note:
This project demonstrates how to concatenate characters from a *char[]* array into a *String* using the + operator in Arduino. It's an excellent example for beginners to understand both character arrays and string manipulation using loops.

Chapter Summary

In this chapter, we covered different types of operators that are essential in Arduino programming for ESP32/ESP8266:

- **Arithmetic Operators**:
  - **Addition (+), Subtraction (-), Multiplication (*), Division (/), Modulo (%)**: Used to perform basic mathematical operations. These operators are fundamental for calculations, such as scaling values, computing totals, or finding remainders.
- **Comparison Operators**:
  - **Equal To (==), Not Equal To (!=), Greater Than (>), Less Than (<), Greater Than or Equal To (>=), Less Than or Equal To (<=)**: Used to compare two values and determine relationships, such as equality or which value is larger. These operators are essential for decision-making in conditional statements.
- **Logical Operators**:
  - **Logical AND (&&), Logical OR (||), Logical NOT (!)**: Used to combine multiple conditions in control structures like if statements. Logical operators allow

for complex decision-making by combining different criteria.

- **Assignment Operators**:
  - **Assignment (=), Addition Assignment (+=), Subtraction Assignment (-=), Multiplication Assignment (*=), Division Assignment (/=)**: Used to assign and update the values of variables. These operators help simplify code when updating variables, such as incrementing counters or applying calculations.

Chapter-5 GPIO I/O operations

This chapter covers the basics of **GPIO (General Purpose Input/Output) operations** in Arduino programming with ESP32 and ESP8266. GPIO pins allow the microcontroller to interface with external devices by reading inputs from sensors or controlling outputs like LEDs, motors, and relays. We discuss configuring pins as input and output, performing digital and analog operations, generating PWM signals, and using interrupts to handle real-time events.

Syntax Table

Topics	Syntax	Simple Example
Input Mode	*pinMode(pin, INPUT);*	*pinMode(2, INPUT); int sensorValue = digitalRead(2);*
Output Mode	*pinMode(pin, OUTPUT);*	*pinMode(13, OUTPUT); digitalWrite(13, HIGH);*
Input Pull-Up	*pinMode(pin, INPUT_PULLUP);*	*pinMode(4, INPUT_PULLUP); int buttonState = digitalRead(4);*

Input Pull-Down	pinMode(pin, INPUT_PULLDOWN);	pinMode(4, INPUT_PULLDOWN); int buttonState = digitalRead(4);
Digital Read	digitalRead(pin);	int buttonState = digitalRead(2);
Digital Write	digitalWrite(pin, value);	digitalWrite(13, HIGH);
Analog Read	analogRead(pin);	int sensorValue = analogRead(34);
Analog Write (DAC)	dacWrite(pin, value);	dacWrite(25, 128);
PWM Output	ledcWrite(channel, value);	ledcSetup(0, 5000, 8); ledcAttachPin(2, 0); ledcWrite(0, 128);
Attach Interrupt	attachInterrupt(pin, function, mode);	attachInterrupt(2, handleInterrupt, FALLING);

1. Pin Configuration

Input Mode:

The *pinMode(pin, INPUT)* function is used to configure a GPIO (General Purpose Input/Output) pin as an input in Arduino. This allows the microcontroller to read signals or data from sensors, switches, or other input devices connected to the pin.

Why is Important
Setting a pin as an input is crucial when you need the microcontroller to read the state of external devices. For instance, if you want to know whether a button is pressed or a sensor detects

an object, configuring the GPIO pin as an input ensures the microcontroller can properly receive this information.

Syntax

```
pinMode(pin, INPUT);
```

Syntax Explanation

pin refers to the GPIO pin number you want to configure.
INPUT is the mode that sets the pin to read incoming signals. When a pin is set as an input, it waits for external voltage levels (either HIGH or LOW).

Code Example

```
int sensorPin = 2;
pinMode(sensorPin, INPUT);
int sensorValue = digitalRead(sensorPin);
Serial.println(sensorValue);
```

Notes

- When a pin is set to *INPUT*, it becomes high-impedance, meaning it draws very little current and can easily detect changes in voltage levels.
- Using *pinMode(pin, INPUT_PULLUP)* enables an internal pull-up resistor, which helps in reading digital inputs without needing an external resistor.

Warnings

- If the input pin is left floating (not connected to anything), it can pick up noise, leading to unreliable readings. It's recommended to use a pull-up or pull-down resistor to ensure the pin has a stable signal.
- Make sure that the voltage levels applied to the pin are within the acceptable range of the microcontroller (typically 3.3V for ESP32/ESP8266), or you risk damaging the chip.

Output Mode:

The *pinMode(pin, OUTPUT)* function configures a GPIO (General Purpose Input/Output) pin as an output. This allows the microcontroller to send signals, such as turning on an LED or controlling a motor, to external devices.

Why is Important
Setting a pin as an output is essential when the microcontroller needs to control external devices like LEDs, motors, relays, or other hardware components. It enables the microcontroller to send HIGH or LOW signals to these devices, effectively controlling their on/off states or other operations.

Syntax

```
pinMode(pin, OUTPUT);
```

Syntax Explanation
pin refers to the GPIO pin number you want to configure. *OUTPUT* is the mode that allows the pin to send signals out to external devices. The pin can be set to either HIGH (on) or LOW (off) using the *digitalWrite* function after being configured as an output.

Code Example

```
int ledPin = 13;
pinMode(ledPin, OUTPUT);
digitalWrite(ledPin, HIGH); // Turns the LED on
delay(1000);
digitalWrite(ledPin, LOW); // Turns the LED off
```

Notes

- When a pin is set to *OUTPUT*, it can deliver a voltage to connected devices, typically 3.3V for ESP32/ESP8266.

- After setting a pin as output, you can control its state using *digitalWrite(pin, HIGH)* to send a high signal (turn on), or *digitalWrite(pin, LOW)* to send a low signal (turn off).

Warnings

- Make sure the external device connected to the pin doesn't exceed the microcontroller's current and voltage limits, or it could damage the pin or the microcontroller. Typically, ESP32/ESP8266 pins can safely source/sink around 12mA.
- Be cautious of using output pins with devices that require more current or voltage than the pin can handle. You may need additional components like transistors or relays to safely control higher-power devices.

Input Pull-Up:

The *pinMode(pin, INPUT_PULLUP)* function configures a GPIO pin as an input and activates the internal pull-up resistor. This allows the pin to read digital signals and prevents the input from floating by defaulting to a HIGH state when not connected to anything.

Why is Important
Using *INPUT_PULLUP* is important when you need to read the state of a button, switch, or sensor without adding an external pull-up resistor. The internal pull-up resistor ensures that the pin is not left floating (which could cause unreliable readings) and defaults to HIGH unless it's actively pulled to LOW by an external connection.

Syntax

```
pinMode(pin, INPUT_PULLUP);
```

Syntax Explanation
pin is the GPIO pin number you want to configure.

INPUT_PULLUP sets the pin as an input and enables the microcontroller's internal pull-up resistor, ensuring the pin defaults to HIGH unless actively pulled LOW.

Code Example

```
int buttonPin = 4;
pinMode(buttonPin, INPUT_PULLUP);
int buttonState = digitalRead(buttonPin);
if (buttonState == LOW) { // Button is pressed (pulled LOW)
Serial.println("Button Pressed");
} else { // Button is not pressed (HIGH by default)
Serial.println("Button Not Pressed");
}
```

Notes

- When using *INPUT_PULLUP*, the default state of the pin is HIGH due to the internal pull-up resistor. This means you should design your logic accordingly: the button press or signal will pull the pin to LOW when activated.
- No need for an external pull-up resistor, making wiring simpler for projects involving buttons or switches.

Warnings

- Keep in mind that the logic is inverted when using *INPUT_PULLUP*: LOW indicates the active state (e.g., button pressed), and HIGH indicates the inactive state (e.g., button not pressed).
- Ensure that the external circuit or device connected to the input can properly pull the pin to LOW when required, as the internal pull-up resistor will keep it HIGH by default.

Input Pull-Down:

The *pinMode(pin, INPUT_PULLDOWN)* function configures a GPIO pin as an input and activates the internal pull-down resistor. This ensures the pin defaults to a LOW state unless it is actively pulled to HIGH by an external connection.

Why is Important

Using *INPUT_PULLDOWN* is crucial when you want to ensure that the pin reads LOW by default, preventing a floating pin (which could lead to unreliable readings). It simplifies circuit design by avoiding the need for an external pull-down resistor when reading signals like button presses or sensor states.

Syntax

```
pinMode(pin, INPUT_PULLDOWN);
```

Syntax Explanation

pin refers to the GPIO pin number you want to configure. *INPUT_PULLDOWN* sets the pin as an input and enables the internal pull-down resistor, ensuring the pin defaults to LOW unless pulled HIGH by an external source.

Code Example

```
int buttonPin = 4;
pinMode(buttonPin, INPUT_PULLDOWN);
int buttonState = digitalRead(buttonPin);
if (buttonState == HIGH) { // Button is pressed (pulled HIGH)
Serial.println("Button Pressed");
} else { // Button is not pressed (LOW by default)
Serial.println("Button Not Pressed");
}
```

Notes

- When using *INPUT_PULLDOWN*, the pin will be in a LOW state by default due to the internal pull-down resistor. This means you will need an external source (like a button press) to pull the pin HIGH when necessary.
- This configuration simplifies the wiring setup by eliminating the need for external pull-down resistors, which would normally be required to keep the pin in a stable state when not connected to an external signal.

Warnings

- Not all microcontrollers support *INPUT_PULLDOWN* natively. Make sure your specific board (such as ESP32/ESP8266) supports this mode.
- Ensure the external circuit or device can pull the pin to HIGH when required, as the internal pull-down resistor will keep the pin LOW by default.

2. Digital I/O Operations

Digital Read:

The *digitalRead(pin)* function reads the digital state of a specified input pin on the microcontroller. The state will either be *HIGH* (when the pin receives a voltage signal) or *LOW* (when no signal or a ground signal is present).

Why is Important
digitalRead(pin) is essential for detecting the state of digital input devices like buttons, switches, and sensors. It allows your microcontroller to know whether a connected device is in an active (HIGH) or inactive (LOW) state and respond accordingly in your code.

Syntax

```
digitalRead(pin);
```

Syntax Explanation
pin refers to the number of the GPIO pin you want to read from. The function will return either *HIGH* or *LOW* based on the voltage level detected on that pin.

Code Example

```
int buttonPin = 2;
pinMode(buttonPin, INPUT);
```

```
int buttonState = digitalRead(buttonPin);
if (buttonState == HIGH) { // Button is pressed
Serial.println("Button Pressed");
} else { // Button is not pressed
Serial.println("Button Not Pressed");
}
```

Notes

- The pin must be configured as an input using *pinMode(pin, INPUT)* before calling *digitalRead(pin)*.
- The function is typically used with digital devices that operate in a binary fashion, such as buttons or sensors that provide HIGH or LOW signals.

Warnings

- If the pin is not connected or left floating, the readings may be unpredictable. Use an internal or external pull-up or pull-down resistor to ensure stable readings.
- Make sure the pin you're reading from is not set as an output, as reading from an output pin may cause confusion or conflicts in your program logic.

Digital Write:

The *digitalWrite(pin, value)* function sets the state of a specified digital pin to either *HIGH* (sending voltage) or *LOW* (grounding the pin). This function is used to control external devices such as LEDs, relays, or motors by changing the voltage on the pin.

Why is Important

The *digitalWrite(pin, value)* function is critical for controlling output devices connected to your microcontroller. It allows you to turn components on or off, or toggle between two states, making it essential in automation and control systems.

Syntax

```
digitalWrite(pin, value);
```

Syntax Explanation

pin refers to the GPIO pin number where you want to set the state. *value* can either be *HIGH* (to turn the pin on or set it to a high voltage level) or *LOW* (to turn the pin off or set it to ground).

Code Example

```
int ledPin = 13;
pinMode(ledPin, OUTPUT);
digitalWrite(ledPin, HIGH); // Turns the LED on
delay(1000);
digitalWrite(ledPin, LOW); // Turns the LED off
delay(1000);
```

Notes

- The pin must be configured as an *OUTPUT* using *pinMode(pin, OUTPUT)* before calling *digitalWrite(pin, value)*.
- Use *digitalWrite* to control digital devices like LEDs, motors, or relays by sending either a HIGH or LOW signal.

Warnings

- Avoid using *digitalWrite* on pins that are configured as inputs, as this may lead to unexpected behavior.
- Be cautious about the current requirements of the devices connected to the pin. Driving high-current loads directly from a pin may damage the microcontroller; use relays, transistors, or MOSFETs for high-power components.

3. Analog I/O Operations

Analog Read:

The *analogRead(pin)* function reads an analog voltage value from a specified pin and converts it into a digital value using the ADC (Analog-to-Digital Converter). On the ESP32/ESP8266, it provides a 12-bit resolution, meaning the reading will range from 0 (0V) to 4095 (maximum voltage, typically 3.3V).

Why is Important

analogRead(pin) is essential for reading sensors or inputs that provide a variable voltage. This includes temperature sensors, light sensors, potentiometers, or any other analog input. It allows the microcontroller to interpret varying signals and act upon them.

Syntax

```
analogRead(pin);
```

Syntax Explanation

pin refers to the GPIO pin number that supports analog input (A0 on ESP8266 or any ADC-capable pin on ESP32). The function returns a value between 0 and 4095 based on the input voltage level.

Code Example

```
int sensorPin = 34; // Pin for analog sensor on ESP32
int sensorValue = analogRead(sensorPin);
Serial.println(sensorValue); // Prints the analog value (0-4095)
```

Notes

- The ADC resolution is 12-bit, which gives values from 0 to 4095. The range corresponds to the input voltage, where 0 is 0V, and 4095 corresponds to the reference voltage (typically 3.3V on ESP32/ESP8266).
- Some pins may have noise or limitations, so it's recommended to check the microcontroller's documentation for the best pins to use for analog input.

Warnings

- Ensure the input voltage to the analog pin does not exceed the maximum allowable voltage (typically 3.3V). Exceeding this limit can damage the pin or the microcontroller.
- Not all GPIO pins on the ESP32 or ESP8266 support analog input. Make sure you are using the correct pin for analog readings (e.g., A0 on ESP8266 or an ADC-capable pin on ESP32).

Analog Write (DAC):

The *dacWrite(pin, value)* function allows you to output an analog voltage on pins with a built-in DAC (Digital-to-Analog Converter), available on pins 25 and 26 of the ESP32. This function converts a digital value (ranging from 0 to 255) into an analog voltage between 0 and 3.3V.

Why is Important
dacWrite(pin, value) is important for controlling devices that require variable voltage, such as audio signals, LED dimming, or motor control. Instead of just switching between ON and OFF (like digital pins), it allows you to output a range of voltages, offering finer control over connected components.

Syntax

```
dacWrite(pin, value);
```

Syntax Explanation
pin is the GPIO number (either 25 or 26) where the DAC output is available.
value is a number between 0 and 255, where 0 corresponds to 0V and 255 corresponds to the maximum output voltage (typically 3.3V).

Code Example

```
int outputPin = 25;
dacWrite(outputPin, 128); // Outputs a voltage roughly halfway between
0 and 3.3V
```

Notes

- The DAC resolution is 8-bit, meaning the values can range from 0 to 255, corresponding to an analog output voltage between 0V and 3.3V.
- This function is only available on specific pins (25 and 26) on the ESP32, as these are the pins equipped with DAC capabilities.

Warnings

- Only use pins 25 or 26 for *dacWrite*, as other pins do not support analog voltage output.
- Ensure that the connected device is compatible with the analog voltage range produced by the DAC, or it may not work correctly or could be damaged.

4. PWM Output

PWM Output:

The *ledcWrite(channel, value)* function generates a PWM (Pulse Width Modulation) signal on a specific GPIO pin. PWM is a technique where the signal alternates between HIGH and LOW, controlling the power delivered to devices like LEDs or motors by adjusting the duty cycle (the proportion of time the signal is HIGH).

Why is Important
PWM is important for controlling the brightness of LEDs, the speed of motors, and other devices that require analog-like control using digital pins. Since digital pins can only be HIGH or LOW, PWM simulates a varying voltage by changing the percentage of time the pin is HIGH within each cycle, giving finer control over devices.

Syntax

```
ledcWrite(channel, value);
```

Syntax Explanation

channel refers to the PWM channel number (0 to 15 on ESP32), which allows for independent control of up to 16 PWM outputs. *value* is the duty cycle of the PWM signal, with values ranging from 0 (always LOW) to 255 (always HIGH), representing the proportion of time the signal remains HIGH during each cycle.

Code Example

```
int ledPin = 2;
ledcSetup(0, 5000, 8); // Set up PWM channel 0 at 5kHz with 8-bit
resolution (0-255)
ledcAttachPin(ledPin, 0); // Attach pin 2 to PWM channel 0
ledcWrite(0, 128); // Set PWM duty cycle to 50% (halfway between 0 and
255)
```

Notes

- The ESP32 has 16 independent PWM channels, allowing you to control multiple devices simultaneously with different frequencies and duty cycles.
- PWM is often used to control the brightness of LEDs or the speed of motors by adjusting the power delivered over time.

Warnings

- Be mindful of the connected device's power requirements. Even though PWM modulates power, excessive current or voltage may damage devices like LEDs or motors. Use resistors or drivers where necessary.
- Ensure the selected PWM frequency and duty cycle are appropriate for the connected device, as incorrect settings could result in inefficient control or device malfunction.

5. Interrupt Handling

Attach Interrupt:

The *attachInterrupt(pin, function, mode)* function attaches an interrupt to a specific GPIO pin. An interrupt allows the microcontroller to immediately respond to an event, such as a change in the state of a pin (from HIGH to LOW or vice versa), without continuously polling the pin.

Why is Important
Interrupts are crucial for time-sensitive applications where immediate action is required. For example, when reading data from sensors or responding to external signals, interrupts enable the microcontroller to focus on other tasks and only react when necessary, making the program more efficient and responsive.

Syntax

```
attachInterrupt(pin, function, mode);
```

Syntax Explanation
pin is the GPIO pin number to which the interrupt is attached.
function is the name of the function that will be called when the interrupt occurs.
mode specifies when the interrupt should trigger. Common modes include:

- *RISING* (trigger when the pin changes from LOW to HIGH),
- *FALLING* (trigger when the pin changes from HIGH to LOW),
- *CHANGE* (trigger when the pin changes in either direction),
- *HIGH* or *LOW* (trigger when the pin is in a constant HIGH or LOW state).

Code Example

```
int buttonPin = 2;
volatile bool buttonPressed = false;
```

```
void IRAM_ATTR handleInterrupt() {
buttonPressed = true;
}
void setup() {
pinMode(buttonPin, INPUT_PULLUP);
attachInterrupt(digitalPinToInterrupt(buttonPin), handleInterrupt,
FALLING);
}
void loop() {
if (buttonPressed) {
Serial.println("Button Pressed!");
buttonPressed = false;
}
}
```

Notes

- Interrupts can be extremely useful in situations where the microcontroller needs to respond immediately to an event, such as button presses or sensor inputs, without continuously checking the state of the pin in the main loop.
- Use *volatile* variables in interrupt service routines to ensure the value is updated correctly when used in the main code.

Warnings

- Keep the code inside the interrupt handler (the function called by the interrupt) as short and fast as possible, since interrupts stop the normal execution of the code.
- Interrupts can sometimes cause unexpected behavior if not carefully managed. Avoid using functions like *delay()* or *Serial.print()* inside interrupt service routines, as these can cause timing issues or deadlocks.

Project- 1.LED Toggle with Button Press for Arduino ESP32/ESP8266

Use a boolean variable to track the LED's state. When a button is pressed (using digitalRead()), an if-else statement will check the button state and toggle the LED using digitalWrite(). The LED's state is toggled by applying the logical NOT operator (!) with the assignment operator (=) to switch between on and off.

Requirement:

- ESP32 or ESP8266 board
- LED
- Push button
- Resistor (10kΩ for the button)

Circuit Connection:

1. Connect the LED anode (+) to a GPIO pin (e.g., GPIO 2), and the cathode (-) to GND.
2. Connect one side of the button to a GPIO pin (e.g., GPIO 4) and the other side to GND.
3. Add a pull-up resistor (10kΩ) between the button pin and 3.3V to ensure a stable signal.

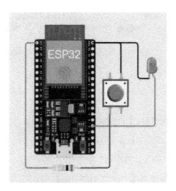

Circuit Analysis:
The button state is read using *digitalRead()*. When the button is pressed, it triggers an *if-else* statement that checks the button's state. The LED state is toggled using the *!LED_state* logic, and the *digitalWrite()* function updates the LED accordingly.

How it works:

1. A *boolean* variable is used to track whether the LED is on or off.

2. The button's state is checked using *digitalRead()*.
3. When the button is pressed, an *if-else* statement toggles the LED's state using *!LED_state*.
4. The LED is turned on or off based on the current state, using *digitalWrite()*.

Code:

```
boolean LED_state = false;
int buttonPin = 4;
int LEDPin = 2;
void setup() {
    pinMode(buttonPin, INPUT_PULLUP);
    pinMode(LEDPin, OUTPUT);
}
void loop() {
    if (digitalRead(buttonPin) == LOW) {
        LED_state = !LED_state;
        digitalWrite(LEDPin, LED_state);
        delay(200); // Debouncing delay
    }
}
```

Code Walkthrough:

- *boolean LED_state = false;* initializes the LED state as off.
- *pinMode(buttonPin, INPUT_PULLUP);* sets the button pin as an input with an internal pull-up resistor.
- *pinMode(LEDPin, OUTPUT);* sets the LED pin as an output.
- The *if-else* statement checks if the button is pressed (*digitalRead(buttonPin) == LOW*). If true, the *LED_state* is toggled using *LED_state = !LED_state;*.
- *digitalWrite(LEDPin, LED_state);* changes the LED's state based on the toggled value.
- *delay(200);* is added to debounce the button press, avoiding multiple toggles with a single press.

Note:

This project demonstrates how to use a button to toggle an LED using a *boolean* variable, conditional logic with *if-else*, and GPIO I/O functions like *digitalRead()* and *digitalWrite()*. It's an ideal beginner project for understanding hardware control and logic operations.

Project- 2 .Button Press Counter with LED Indicator for Arduino ESP32/ESP8266

Use an *int* variable to count the number of button presses (using *digitalRead()*). In each iteration of a *for* loop, increment the counter using the ++ operator. The *modulus (%)* operator is used to check if the counter is even or odd, and the LED is turned on or off (using *digitalWrite()*) based on the result.

Requirement:

- ESP32 or ESP8266 board
- LED
- Push button
- Resistor (10kΩ for the button)

Circuit Connection:

1. Connect the LED anode (+) to a GPIO pin (e.g., GPIO 2), and the cathode (-) to GND.
2. Connect one side of the button to a GPIO pin (e.g., GPIO 4) and the other side to GND.
3. Add a pull-up resistor (10kΩ) between the button pin and 3.3V to ensure stable input.

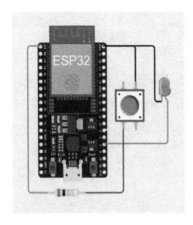

Circuit Analysis:

The button's state is read using *digitalRead()*. Every time the button is pressed, the counter is incremented using ++. The *modulus (%)* operator checks if the counter is even or odd, and the LED is turned on or off based on the result. Even counts turn the LED on, and odd counts turn it off.

How it works:

1. An *int* variable tracks the button press count.
2. The button state is checked with *digitalRead()*.
3. When the button is pressed, the counter is incremented using the ++ operator.
4. A *for* loop cycles through, and the % operator checks whether the count is even or odd.
5. The LED is controlled by *digitalWrite()*, turning it on if the count is even and off if the count is odd.

Code:

```
int buttonPin = 4;
int LEDPin = 2;
int pressCount = 0;
void setup() {
    pinMode(buttonPin, INPUT_PULLUP);
    pinMode(LEDPin, OUTPUT);
}
void loop() {
```

```
    if (digitalRead(buttonPin) == LOW) {
        pressCount++;
        for (int i = 0; i < pressCount; i++) {
            if (pressCount % 2 == 0) {
                digitalWrite(LEDPin, HIGH); // Even: LED ON
            } else {
                digitalWrite(LEDPin, LOW); // Odd: LED OFF
            }
        }
        delay(500); // Debouncing delay
    }
}
```

Code Walkthrough:

- *pressCount++* increments the button press count each time the button is pressed.
- The *for* loop cycles through the number of presses, evaluating whether the count is even or odd using *pressCount % 2 == 0*.
- If the count is even, *digitalWrite(LEDPin, HIGH);* turns the LED on. If odd, *digitalWrite(LEDPin, LOW);* turns the LED off.
- *delay(500);* adds a delay between button presses to debounce the button and prevent false readings.

Note:
This project demonstrates how to count button presses and use the *modulus (%)* operator to determine whether a number is even or odd. The project uses a *for* loop and *if* conditions to control the LED's behavior based on the button press count.

Project- 3. PWM LED Brightness Control with Potentiometer for Arduino ESP32/ESP8266

Use a potentiometer to control the brightness of an LED using PWM (Pulse Width Modulation). The potentiometer's analog input is read using *analogRead()*, scaled with a *float* variable, and the LED brightness is adjusted with *analogWrite()* based on the potentiometer's position.

Requirement:

- ESP32 or ESP8266 board
- LED
- Potentiometer
- Resistor (220Ω for the LED)

Circuit Connection:

1. Connect the potentiometer's middle pin to an analog input pin (e.g., GPIO 34).
2. Connect one side of the potentiometer to 3.3V and the other side to GND.
3. Connect the LED anode (+) to a PWM-capable GPIO pin (e.g., GPIO 2) and the cathode (-) to GND.
4. Add a 220Ω resistor in series with the LED to limit current.

Circuit Analysis:

The potentiometer's analog value is read using *analogRead()*, which returns a value between 0 and 4095. This value is then scaled using a *float* variable to match the PWM range (0-255) for the ESP32. The *analogWrite()* function adjusts the LED's brightness based on this scaled value.

How it works:

1. The analog value from the potentiometer is read using *analogRead()*.

2. The value is stored in an *int* variable.
3. A *float* variable is used to scale the potentiometer's value to match the PWM range.
4. A *while* loop continuously reads the potentiometer value and adjusts the LED brightness using *analogWrite()*.

Code:

```
int potPin = 34;
int LEDPin = 2;
int potValue = 0;
float brightness = 0.0;
void setup() {
    pinMode(LEDPin, OUTPUT);
}
void loop() {
    while (true) {
        potValue = analogRead(potPin);
        brightness = potValue / 16.0; // Scale 0-4095 to 0-255
        analogWrite(LEDPin, (int)brightness); // Set LED brightness
        delay(10); // Small delay for smoother transition
    }
}
```

Code Walkthrough:

- *analogRead(potPin)* reads the analog value from the potentiometer (0-4095).
- The *float* variable *brightness* scales this value by dividing it by 16.0 to match the PWM range (0-255).
- *analogWrite(LEDPin, (int)brightness);* adjusts the LED brightness based on the scaled value.
- A *while* loop continuously updates the LED brightness as the potentiometer is adjusted.

Note:
This project shows how to control the brightness of an LED using a potentiometer and PWM on the ESP32/ESP8266. The potentiometer provides an analog input, which is scaled to control the LED brightness in real-time.

Chapter Summary

In this chapter, we covered different GPIO operations for controlling and interfacing with external devices on ESP32/ESP8266:

1. **Pin Configuration**:
   - **Input Mode (*pinMode(pin, INPUT)*)**: Configures the pin to read signals from sensors or switches. This mode is crucial for reading digital input values.
   - **Output Mode (*pinMode(pin, OUTPUT)*)**: Configures the pin to send signals, such as turning on an LED or controlling a motor.
   - **Input Pull-Up (*pinMode(pin, INPUT_PULLUP)*)**: Configures the pin as input with an internal pull-up resistor, useful for reading buttons without needing an external resistor.
   - **Input Pull-Down (*pinMode(pin, INPUT_PULLDOWN)*)**: Configures the pin as input with an internal pull-down resistor, ensuring the pin reads LOW by default until pulled HIGH by an external source.
2. **Digital I/O Operations**:
   - **Digital Read (*digitalRead(pin)*)**: Reads the current state (HIGH or LOW) of an input pin. It is essential for detecting states like button presses or sensor triggers.
   - **Digital Write (*digitalWrite(pin, value)*)**: Sets an output pin to HIGH or LOW, which controls devices such as LEDs and relays.
3. **Analog I/O Operations**:
   - **Analog Read (*analogRead(pin)*)**: Reads an analog voltage (0 to 3.3V) from a specified pin and converts it to a digital value (0 to 4095). Useful for reading variable inputs like sensors.
   - **Analog Write (DAC) (*dacWrite(pin, value)*)**: Outputs an analog voltage using the built-in DAC on specific pins (25 or 26) of the ESP32, suitable for devices that require variable voltage control.
4. **PWM Output**:

- **PWM Output (*ledcWrite(channel, value)*)**: Generates a PWM signal, allowing for control of brightness of LEDs or speed of motors. The PWM signal simulates an analog output by adjusting the duty cycle of the digital signal.

5. **Interrupt Handling**:
   - **Attach Interrupt (*attachInterrupt(pin, function, mode)*)**: Attaches an interrupt to a GPIO pin, allowing the microcontroller to respond immediately to an event, such as a change in the pin's state. Interrupts are crucial for time-sensitive tasks, allowing efficient and responsive programming.

Chapter-6 Timing and Delays

This chapter covers different methods for managing timing and delays in Arduino programming for ESP32/ESP8266. Timing is crucial for tasks like controlling LEDs, reading sensor data, or managing communication protocols. We explore basic delays using the *delay()* function, non-blocking timing using the *millis()* and *micros()* functions, and microsecond delays using *delayMicroseconds()*. Understanding these functions will help you create efficient programs for managing time-sensitive tasks.

Syntax Table

Topics	Syntax	Simple Example
Delay Function	*delay(ms);*	*delay(1000);*
Millis Function	*millis();*	*unsigned long currentMillis = millis();*
Micros Function	*micros();*	*unsigned long currentTime = micros();*
Delay in Microseconds	*delayMicroseconds(us);*	*delayMicroseconds(1000);*

1. Basic Delays

Delay Function: delay(ms)
The *delay(ms)* function pauses the execution of the program for a specified number of milliseconds. During this time, no other code is executed.

Why is Important
The *delay(ms)* function is useful when you need to introduce a pause in your program, such as waiting for a sensor to stabilize or creating a time gap between events (like blinking an LED). It's a

simple way to control the timing in your program without complicated logic.

Syntax

```
delay(ms);
```

Syntax Explanation

ms is the number of milliseconds (1 second = 1000 milliseconds) the program should pause. During this time, the microcontroller will not execute any further instructions.

Code Example

```
int ledPin = 13;
pinMode(ledPin, OUTPUT);
while (true) {
digitalWrite(ledPin, HIGH); // Turn LED on
delay(1000); // Wait for 1 second
digitalWrite(ledPin, LOW); // Turn LED off
delay(1000); // Wait for 1 second
}
```

Notes

- The *delay()* function is simple to use but blocks the execution of other code while the delay is active, meaning the program can't do anything else during this time.
- It's useful in situations where precise timing is not critical, or you want to create simple delays in the execution of your program.

Warnings

- Since *delay()* blocks the entire program, it can cause issues in time-sensitive applications where other tasks need to be executed during the delay period. For these cases, non-blocking alternatives like *millis()* or *timers* are often preferred.

- Avoid using *delay()* in programs with multiple tasks or where real-time responses are needed, as it can lead to poor performance or unresponsiveness.

2. Non-blocking Timing

Millis Function: millis()

The *millis()* function returns the number of milliseconds that have passed since the ESP32 was powered on or reset. Unlike *delay()*, it does not stop the program from running, making it useful for timing mechanisms that don't block other tasks.

Why is Important
millis() is important for creating non-blocking delays, allowing the microcontroller to perform other tasks while still tracking elapsed time. It is widely used in applications where multiple tasks need to run simultaneously, like controlling LEDs while also reading sensor data, without pausing the entire program.

Syntax

```
millis();
```

Syntax Explanation
The *millis()* function does not require any arguments. It simply returns an unsigned long integer representing the number of milliseconds since the device was powered on or reset.

Code Example

```
unsigned long previousMillis = 0;
const long interval = 1000; // Interval of 1 second
void setup() {
pinMode(LED_BUILTIN, OUTPUT);
}
void loop() {
unsigned long currentMillis = millis();
if (currentMillis - previousMillis >= interval) {
```

```
previousMillis = currentMillis;
digitalWrite(LED_BUILTIN, !digitalRead(LED_BUILTIN)); // Toggle LED
}
}
```

Notes

- *millis()* is extremely useful for implementing non-blocking timing. It allows your program to keep track of time without stopping other tasks, unlike *delay()*.
- It counts up to approximately 50 days before it resets, but this is rarely an issue unless your system runs continuously for that duration.

Warnings

- The value returned by *millis()* will eventually overflow (reset to 0) after approximately 50 days. Plan for this in long-running applications, although it typically doesn't cause issues in most programs.
- Be sure to use *unsigned long* variables when working with *millis()* to avoid overflow issues and incorrect time comparisons.

Micros Function: micros()

The *micros()* function returns the number of microseconds (1 second = 1,000,000 microseconds) that have passed since the ESP32 was powered on or reset. This is useful for precise timing operations that require more accuracy than the *millis()* function.

Why is Important

micros() is essential when you need higher resolution timing than what *millis()* offers. It is useful for tasks requiring precise control, such as generating signals, measuring time intervals in microcontroller communication protocols, or implementing time-critical functions like pulse-width modulation (PWM).

Syntax

```
micros();
```

Syntax Explanation

The *micros()* function returns an unsigned long integer representing the number of microseconds since the ESP32 was powered on or reset. No arguments are required.

Code Example

```
unsigned long startTime;
void setup() {
Serial.begin(115200);
startTime = micros();
}
void loop() {
unsigned long currentTime = micros();
if (currentTime - startTime >= 1000000) { // 1 second = 1,000,000
microseconds
Serial.println("1 second has passed");
startTime = currentTime;
}
}
```

Notes

- *micros()* provides a much higher resolution than *millis()*, making it ideal for tasks that require microsecond-level accuracy.
- Similar to *millis()*, *micros()* counts upwards and will eventually overflow. However, this occurs after approximately 71 minutes, compared to the 50-day overflow period for *millis()*.

Warnings

- The *micros()* function, like *millis()*, will eventually overflow, resetting to 0 after around 71 minutes. In most cases, this isn't an issue, but it should be accounted for in time-sensitive applications.

- Be sure to use *unsigned long* variables when working with *micros()* to avoid overflow issues and ensure accurate time calculations.

3. Microsecond Delays

Delay in Microseconds

The *delayMicroseconds(us)* function pauses the execution of the program for a specified number of microseconds (1 second = 1,000,000 microseconds). This function is useful when precise, short delays are needed in time-critical operations.

Why is Important
delayMicroseconds(us) is crucial for tasks requiring precise, short delays in the microsecond range. It's especially useful in low-level communication protocols, generating specific timing signals, or interacting with sensors and devices that require fast, accurate timing.

Syntax

```
delayMicroseconds(us);
```

Syntax Explanation
us refers to the number of microseconds for which the program should pause. The function halts program execution for this duration, allowing for precise timing control in operations requiring brief pauses.

Code Example

```
int ledPin = 13;
pinMode(ledPin, OUTPUT);
while (true) {
digitalWrite(ledPin, HIGH); // Turn LED on
```

```
delayMicroseconds(1000); // Wait for 1000 microseconds (1 millisecond)
digitalWrite(ledPin, LOW); // Turn LED off
delayMicroseconds(1000); // Wait for 1000 microseconds (1 millisecond)
}
```

Notes

- *delayMicroseconds()* is particularly useful for generating precise time delays in the microsecond range. It's important for tasks like signal generation, managing communication timing, and interfacing with time-sensitive sensors.
- It provides a more precise timing than *delay()*, which only works at the millisecond level.

Warnings

- The precision of *delayMicroseconds()* may vary slightly depending on the clock speed of the microcontroller and the overall system load.
- Like *delay()*, this function pauses the entire program execution, meaning no other code will run during the delay period. Avoid using it for long delays, as it can block other important tasks.

Project- 1.LED Blink with Variable Time Interval for Arduino ESP32/ESP8266

Create a project where an LED blinks on and off, with a variable time interval between blinks. An int variable stores the time interval, and the blink speed is adjusted by changing the delay time between the LED's on and off states using digitalWrite() and delay().

Requirement:

- ESP32 or ESP8266 board
- LED
- Resistor (220Ω for the LED)

Circuit Connection:

1. Connect the LED anode (+) to a GPIO pin (e.g., GPIO 2) and the cathode (-) to GND.
2. Add a 220Ω resistor in series with the LED to limit current.

Circuit Analysis:

The project uses an *int* variable to set the time interval between the LED's on and off states. The *if-else* structure is used to toggle the LED state using *digitalWrite()*. The delay between the blinks is controlled by *delay(interval)*, and the interval is adjusted dynamically.

How it works:

1. An *int* variable is used to store the time interval between the LED on and off states.
2. The LED state is toggled using *digitalWrite()*.
3. The time interval is adjusted by increasing or decreasing the delay time with *delay(interval)*.
4. The *if-else* structure controls the logic for turning the LED on and off.

Code:

```
int LEDPin = 2;
int interval = 500; // Initial interval of 500ms
void setup() {
    pinMode(LEDPin, OUTPUT);
}
void loop() {
    if (interval > 1000) {
        interval = 500; // Reset interval to 500ms if it exceeds 1000ms
    } else {
        interval += 100; // Increase interval by 100ms each cycle
    }
    digitalWrite(LEDPin, HIGH); // Turn LED on
    delay(interval); // Wait for 'interval' milliseconds
    digitalWrite(LEDPin, LOW); // Turn LED off
    delay(interval); // Wait for 'interval' milliseconds
}
```

Code Walkthrough:

- *int interval = 500;* sets the initial blink interval to 500 milliseconds.
- In the *if-else* structure, if the interval exceeds 1000ms, it resets to 500ms. Otherwise, the interval increases by 100ms with each cycle.
- *digitalWrite(LEDPin, HIGH);* turns the LED on, followed by a delay of the current interval.
- *digitalWrite(LEDPin, LOW);* turns the LED off, and another delay is applied, controlling the blink speed.

Note:

This project demonstrates how to control an LED's blink rate with a variable time interval using a combination of *digitalWrite()*, *delay()*, and an *int* variable for timing. The interval dynamically increases within a range, creating a progressively slower blink effect.

Project- 2. Button Debounce with LED Toggle for Arduino ESP32/ESP8266

Object:

Implement a button debounce mechanism to reliably toggle an LED on or off when a button is pressed. Use *millis()* to track the time and prevent false triggers. An *unsigned long* variable stores the last time the button was pressed, and *if* conditions with logical operators are used to check the time difference before toggling the LED.

Requirement:

- ESP32 or ESP8266 board
- LED
- Push button
- Resistor (10kΩ for the button)

Circuit Connection:

1. Connect the LED anode (+) to a GPIO pin (e.g., GPIO 2) and the cathode (-) to GND.
2. Connect one side of the button to a GPIO pin (e.g., GPIO 4) and the other side to GND.
3. Add a pull-up resistor (10kΩ) between the button pin and 3.3V.

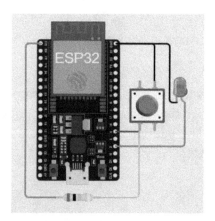

Circuit Analysis:

The button press is read using *digitalRead()*. To avoid multiple triggers from a single press due to bouncing, a debounce delay is implemented using *millis()*. The LED state is toggled only if the time since the last button press exceeds the debounce delay.

How it works:

1. A *boolean* variable is used to track the LED state (on or off).
2. An *unsigned long* variable stores the last time the button was pressed.
3. The *if* condition checks the time difference between the current time (*millis()*) and the last press time. If the difference exceeds the debounce delay, the LED state is toggled.
4. *digitalWrite()* is used to control the LED based on its current state.

Code:

```
int buttonPin = 4;
int LEDPin = 2;
boolean LEDState = false;
unsigned long lastPressTime = 0;
unsigned long debounceDelay = 200; // 200ms debounce delay
void setup() {
    pinMode(buttonPin, INPUT_PULLUP);
    pinMode(LEDPin, OUTPUT);
}
void loop() {
    if (digitalRead(buttonPin) == LOW && (millis() - lastPressTime >
debounceDelay)) {
        LEDState = !LEDState; // Toggle LED state
        digitalWrite(LEDPin, LEDState); // Update LED
        lastPressTime = millis(); // Update the last press time
    }
}
```

Code Walkthrough:

- *boolean LEDState = false;* initializes the LED as off.
- *unsigned long lastPressTime = 0;* stores the last time the button was pressed.

- *if (digitalRead(buttonPin) == LOW && (millis() - lastPressTime > debounceDelay))* checks if the button is pressed and if enough time has passed since the last press to debounce.
- *LEDState = !LEDState;* toggles the LED state between on and off.
- *digitalWrite(LEDPin, LEDState);* sets the LED to its new state.
- *lastPressTime = millis();* updates the time of the last button press.

Note:
This project demonstrates how to implement a debounce mechanism using *millis()* to prevent false triggers when toggling an LED with a button. The debounce delay ensures that only a single toggle occurs with each press, making the button press more reliable.

Chapter Summary

In this chapter, we covered different methods for managing timing in Arduino, including basic delays with *delay()*, non-blocking timing with *millis()* and *micros()*, and microsecond delays using *delayMicroseconds()*. These functions help in implementing precise and effective time management for ESP32/ESP8266-based projects.

Chapter-7 Maths Functions

This chapter covers various math functions in Arduino programming for ESP32/ESP8266. These functions help perform mathematical calculations essential for sensor data processing, decision-making, value mapping, and randomization in different projects. We explore basic math functions like *abs()*, *max()*, and *min()*, value mapping with *map()*, power and square root operations, rounding functions, and generating random numbers.

Syntax Table

Topics	Syntax	Simple Example
Absolute Value	abs(x);	int positiveNum = abs(-5);
Maximum Value	max(x, y);	int largerValue = max(10, 20);
Minimum Value	min(x, y);	int smallerValue = min(10, 20);
Map Value to Range	map(value, fromLow, fromHigh, toLow, toHigh);	int outputValue = map(sensorValue, 0, 1023, 0, 255);
Power	pow(base, exponent);	double result = pow(2, 3);
Square Root	sqrt(x);	double result = sqrt(16);
Round to Nearest	round(x);	int roundedNumber = round(4.6);
Round Up	ceil(x);	int roundedUpNumber = ceil(4.1);
Round Down	floor(x);	int roundedDownNumber = floor(4.9);
Generate Random Number	random(min, max);	int randomValue = random(1, 10);

1. Basic Maths Functions

Absolute Value:

The *abs(x)* function returns the absolute (positive) value of a number *x*. This means that if *x* is a negative number, *abs(x)* will convert it to its positive counterpart, while positive values remain unchanged.

Why is Important
abs(x) is important when you need to ensure that only positive values are used in calculations, regardless of the input. This is useful in many scenarios like measuring distances, working with sensor data, or in algorithms where negative numbers are not meaningful.

Syntax

```
abs(x);
```

Syntax Explanation
x refers to the number or variable for which you want to get the absolute value. The function will return the positive version of *x*, whether it is a positive or negative number.

Code Example

```
int num = -5;
int positiveNum = abs(num);
Serial.println(positiveNum); // Output: 5
```

Notes

- The *abs()* function works with integers as well as floating-point numbers (e.g., -3.14 becomes 3.14).
- This function is widely used in mathematical operations where the direction of a value (positive or negative) doesn't matter, but the magnitude does.

Warnings

- Be mindful that *abs()* does not handle the sign of zero. The function will return 0 if *x* is 0, and no negative zero concept exists in this context.
- If *x* is too large or overflows, the result may not be accurate, particularly with very large negative values on systems with limited data size, like microcontrollers.

Maximum Value:

The *max(x, y)* function returns the larger of two numbers, *x* and *y*. It compares the values and outputs whichever is greater.

Why is Important
max(x, y) is important when you need to compare two numbers and determine which one is larger. This is useful in many programming scenarios, such as finding the highest sensor reading, calculating maximum limits, or determining the best of two values in decision-making processes.

Syntax

```
max(x, y);
```

Syntax Explanation
x and *y* are the two numbers to be compared. The function evaluates both and returns the larger value.

Code Example

```
int a = 10;
int b = 20;
int largerValue = max(a, b);
Serial.println(largerValue); // Output: 20
```

Notes

- *max(x, y)* can be used with integers, floating-point numbers, or any numeric type supported by Arduino.
- This function is commonly used in situations where you need to find the maximum value between two options.

Warnings

- Be cautious of data types when using *max(x, y)*, as mismatches (e.g., comparing an integer with a floating-point number) might result in unexpected behavior or loss of precision.

Minimum Value:

The *min(x, y)* function returns the smaller of two numbers, *x* and *y*. It compares the values and outputs whichever is smaller.

Why is Important
min(x, y) is important when you need to find the lowest of two values. This is useful in scenarios such as finding the minimum sensor reading, setting lower bounds in control algorithms, or determining the least of two values for decision-making processes.

Syntax

```
min(x, y);
```

Syntax Explanation
x and *y* are the two numbers to be compared. The function evaluates both and returns the smaller value.

Code Example

```
int a = 10;
int b = 20;
int smallerValue = min(a, b);
Serial.println(smallerValue); // Output: 10
```

Notes

- *min(x, y)* can be used with integers, floating-point numbers, or any numeric type supported by Arduino.
- This function is often used to enforce lower limits in algorithms or to find the minimum value between two options.

Warnings

- Be mindful of data type compatibility when using *min(x, y)*, as comparing different data types (e.g., integer and float) can lead to loss of precision or unexpected results.

2. Value Mapping

Map Value to Range

The *map(value, fromLow, fromHigh, toLow, toHigh)* function remaps a number from one range to another. It takes an input value from one range (e.g., 0-1023) and scales it proportionally to a new range (e.g., 0-255).

Why is Important
map(value, fromLow, fromHigh, toLow, toHigh) is crucial when you need to convert values from one scale to another. This is particularly useful in situations like reading sensor data (which might have a large range) and mapping it to a smaller range, such as controlling an LED's brightness or motor speed.

Syntax

```
map(value, fromLow, fromHigh, toLow, toHigh);
```

Syntax Explanation

- *value* is the input number you want to remap.
- *fromLow* and *fromHigh* are the bounds of the input range.
- *toLow* and *toHigh* are the bounds of the output range.

The function scales the *value* from the input range to the output range proportionally.

Code Example

```
int sensorValue = analogRead(A0);
int outputValue = map(sensorValue, 0, 1023, 0, 255);
analogWrite(ledPin, outputValue); // Adjust brightness of an LED based
on sensor reading
```

Notes

- The *map()* function does not constrain the output to stay within the *toLow* and *toHigh* range. If the *value* is outside the *fromLow* and *fromHigh* range, the result might be outside the output range as well. Use the *constrain()* function if needed to limit the output range.
- This function is commonly used when working with sensors and actuators that operate on different scales.

Warnings

- Be aware that the *map()* function works with integer values, so fractional values will be truncated. If you need higher precision, additional calculations may be required.
- The *map()* function does not perform any error checking. Ensure that the input and output ranges are correct, or the remapped values may not behave as expected.

3. Power and Square Root

Power:

The *pow(base, exponent)* function raises the *base* to the power of *exponent*, effectively performing a mathematical operation of base^exponent.

Why is Important
pow(base, exponent) is important for performing exponentiation, which is widely used in mathematical calculations, especially in fields like physics, engineering, and data processing. It enables the microcontroller to calculate powers without needing to manually multiply the base multiple times.

Syntax

```
pow(base, exponent);
```

Syntax Explanation
base is the number you want to raise to a power.
exponent is the power to which you want to raise the base.

The function returns the result of base^exponent.

Code Example

```
double result = pow(2, 3);
Serial.println(result); // Output: 8
```

Notes
- The *pow()* function works with floating-point numbers (both base and exponent), allowing it to handle fractional exponents as well as large numbers.
- This function is useful in various mathematical models where powers are required, such as calculating exponential growth, physics formulas, and more.

Warnings

- Be cautious when using *pow()* with large numbers, as it may result in overflow or loss of precision on small microcontrollers like the ESP32 or ESP8266.
- Floating-point calculations can sometimes produce minor inaccuracies due to rounding errors inherent in the way these values are handled in computers.

Square Root:

The *sqrt(x)* function returns the square root of the number *x*. The square root of a number is a value that, when multiplied by itself, gives the original number.

Why is Important
sqrt(x) is important for performing mathematical calculations involving geometry, physics, or any field where square root operations are necessary. It simplifies the process of calculating distances, areas, and other values where the square root is commonly used.

Syntax

```
sqrt(x);
```

Syntax Explanation
x is the number you want to find the square root of. The function returns the square root of *x*.

Code Example

```
double result = sqrt(16);
Serial.println(result); // Output: 4
```

Notes

- The *sqrt()* function works with floating-point numbers, allowing it to handle both whole numbers and decimals.
- It's commonly used in calculations for distance, velocity, and other scientific computations.

Warnings

- The function will return 0 for negative numbers, as the square root of negative numbers is not defined in real numbers (use complex numbers in advanced mathematics for this).
- Be cautious when using *sqrt()* on very large or small values, as the result might lose precision on microcontrollers with limited processing power.

4. Rounding Functions

Round to Nearest:

The *round(x)* function rounds the value of *x* to the nearest whole number. If the fractional part of *x* is 0.5 or greater, it rounds up; otherwise, it rounds down.

Why is Important
round(x) is important when you need to convert a floating-point number to an integer for applications that require whole numbers, such as counting objects, displaying numbers, or controlling hardware with discrete steps.

Syntax

```
round(x);
```

Syntax Explanation
x is the number to be rounded. The function returns the nearest integer based on the fractional part of *x*.

Code Example

```
float number = 4.6;
int roundedNumber = round(number);
Serial.println(roundedNumber); // Output: 5
```

Notes

- The *round()* function works with both positive and negative numbers.
- If the fractional part is exactly 0.5, the function rounds away from zero (i.e., rounds up).

Warnings

- Be cautious when using *round()* with very large floating-point numbers, as rounding can lead to slight precision errors in the result.
- Keep in mind that *round()* returns an integer value, which may truncate the decimal part completely. Use this only when rounding is necessary for your application.

Round Up:

The *ceil(x)* function rounds the value of *x* up to the nearest whole number. Even if the fractional part of *x* is small (e.g., 0.1), it rounds the number up to the next integer.

Why is Important
ceil(x) is important when you need to ensure that a value is always rounded up. This is useful in scenarios where you want to guarantee that the result is not smaller than the actual value, such as allocating resources, handling capacity, or ensuring safe margins in calculations.

Syntax

```
ceil(x);
```

Syntax Explanation
x is the number to be rounded up. The function returns the smallest integer greater than or equal to *x*.

Code Example

```
float number = 4.1;
int roundedUpNumber = ceil(number);
Serial.println(roundedUpNumber); // Output: 5
```

Notes

- The *ceil()* function works with both positive and negative numbers, rounding up towards the nearest integer. For example, *ceil(-4.5)* will return -4.
- This function is useful when you need the next whole number, even if the decimal part is small.

Warnings

- Be mindful of the data type returned by *ceil()*, as it returns a floating-point number. If you need an integer, you may need to explicitly cast the result to an integer.
- Using *ceil()* with very large numbers may result in precision loss on microcontrollers with limited floating-point accuracy.

Round Down:

The *floor(x)* function rounds the value of x down to the nearest whole number. It always rounds towards negative infinity, meaning it discards any fractional part of the number and returns the largest integer less than or equal to x.

Why is Important
floor(x) is important when you need to ensure that a value is always rounded down. This is useful in situations where you want to avoid exceeding a limit or when calculating measurements that must stay within a defined range.

Syntax

```
floor(x);
```

Syntax Explanation

x is the number to be rounded down. The function returns the greatest integer less than or equal to *x*.

Code Example

```
float number = 4.9;
int roundedDownNumber = floor(number);
Serial.println(roundedDownNumber); // Output: 4
```

Notes

- The *floor()* function works with both positive and negative numbers. For example, *floor(-4.5)* will return -5.
- This function is useful when you need to round down, regardless of the fractional part.

Warnings

- The *floor()* function returns a floating-point number, so if you need an integer, you may need to cast the result to an integer.
- Be aware of precision limitations when using *floor()* with very large or small floating-point values, as microcontrollers have limited accuracy with these values.

5. Random Numbers

Generate Random Number:

The *random(min, max)* function generates a random number between the specified *min* (inclusive) and *max* (exclusive). The generated number can be any integer within that range.

Why is Important

random(min, max) is important for creating unpredictable outcomes in your programs. It's widely used in scenarios like randomizing sensor data, creating unique behaviors in interactive systems, and generating unpredictable events in games or simulations.

Syntax

```
random(min, max);
```

Syntax Explanation

min is the lower bound (inclusive) and *max* is the upper bound (exclusive) for the random number. The function returns an integer that falls within this range.

Code Example

```
int randomValue = random(1, 10);
Serial.println(randomValue); // Outputs a random number between 1 and 9
```

Notes

- If you only provide one argument, such as *random(max)*, the function will generate a random number between 0 and *max* (exclusive).
- The randomness of the generated numbers can be improved by using the *randomSeed()* function to seed the random number generator with a more unpredictable value, like a sensor reading.

Warnings

- The upper bound (*max*) is exclusive, meaning the generated random number will always be less than *max*.
- If you don't use *randomSeed()*, the random number sequence will be the same each time the program runs, as the generator starts with the same default seed. Use *randomSeed()* to introduce more variability.

Project- 1. LED Brightness Control with Sinusoidal Wave for Arduino ESP32/ESP8266

Control the brightness of an LED using a sinusoidal wave pattern. The sin() function generates smooth transitions for LED brightness, creating a gradual fade-in and fade-out effect. The sine values are scaled to fit the PWM range (0-255) and adjusted using delay() to control the speed of the fade.

Requirement:

- ESP32 or ESP8266 board
- LED
- Resistor (220Ω for the LED)

Circuit Connection:

1. Connect the LED anode (+) to a PWM-capable GPIO pin (e.g., GPIO 2) and the cathode (-) to GND.
2. Add a 220Ω resistor in series with the LED to limit current.

Circuit Analysis:

The project uses the *sin()* function to create a sinusoidal wave pattern. The sine values range between -1 and 1, so these values are scaled to fit the PWM range of 0 to 255, which controls the LED brightness. A *for* loop iterates through the wave pattern, and *delay()* adjusts the speed of the brightness transition.

How it works:

1. The *sin()* function is used to generate values between -1 and 1.
2. The sine values are scaled to the PWM range (0-255) using arithmetic operations.
3. The LED brightness is controlled by writing the scaled value to the LED using *analogWrite()*.
4. A *for* loop gradually adjusts the brightness by stepping through the sinusoidal values.

Code:

```
int LEDPin = 2;
float brightness = 0.0;
int PWMValue = 0;
int delayTime = 20; // Delay time for controlling the fade speed
void setup() {
    pinMode(LEDPin, OUTPUT);
}
void loop() {
    for (int i = 0; i < 360; i++) { // 360 degrees for a full sine wave
cycle
        brightness = (sin(i * 3.14159 / 180)); // Convert degrees to
radians
        PWMValue = int((brightness + 1) * 127.5); // Scale -1 to 1
range to 0-255
        analogWrite(LEDPin, PWMValue); // Write PWM value to LED
        delay(delayTime); // Control the speed of the fade
    }
}
```

Code Walkthrough:

- *brightness = (sin(i * 3.14159 / 180));* converts the angle *i* from degrees to radians and calculates the sine value.
- *PWMValue = int((brightness + 1) * 127.5);* scales the sine value (-1 to 1) to the PWM range (0-255).
- *analogWrite(LEDPin, PWMValue);* adjusts the brightness of the LED according to the calculated PWM value.

- *delay(delayTime);* introduces a small delay to control the speed of the fade-in and fade-out effect.

Note:

This project demonstrates how to create smooth brightness transitions using a sinusoidal wave with the *sin()* function. The LED fades in and out following a sine wave pattern, providing a smooth visual effect with precise brightness control.

2. Distance Calculation Based on Button Presses for Arduino ESP32/ESP8266

Simulate the calculation of distance using the Pythagorean theorem. Each button press represents movement along an axis (either x or y), and after a series of presses, use the sqrt() function to calculate the distance from the starting point. The result is displayed either via an LED (brightness indicating distance) or on the Serial Monitor.

Requirement:

- ESP32 or ESP8266 board
- LED
- Push button
- Resistor (10kΩ for the button)

Circuit Connection:

1. Connect the LED anode (+) to a PWM-capable GPIO pin (e.g., GPIO 2) and the cathode (-) to GND.
2. Connect one side of the button to a GPIO pin (e.g., GPIO 4) and the other side to GND.
3. Add a pull-up resistor (10kΩ) between the button pin and 3.3V.

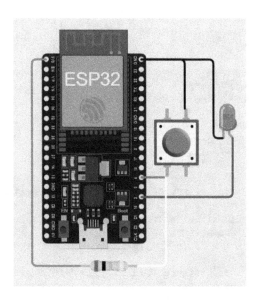

Circuit Analysis:

Every time the button is pressed, the movement along one axis (either x or y) is incremented. Once a set number of presses are completed, the *sqrt()* function is used to calculate the distance using the Pythagorean theorem. The distance is displayed as the brightness of the LED, or the value is printed on the Serial Monitor.

How it works:

1. Two *float* variables are used to track movement along the x and y axes.
2. Each button press increments the movement along one axis.
3. The *sqrt()* function calculates the distance from the starting point using the Pythagorean theorem.
4. The result is displayed on the LED using PWM (brightness indicates distance) or printed via the Serial Monitor.

Code:

```
int buttonPin = 4;
int LEDPin = 2;
float x = 0.0;
float y = 0.0;
float distance = 0.0;
unsigned long lastPressTime = 0;
unsigned long debounceDelay = 200;
void setup() {
    pinMode(buttonPin, INPUT_PULLUP);
    pinMode(LEDPin, OUTPUT);
    Serial.begin(115200);
}
void loop() {
    if (digitalRead(buttonPin) == LOW && (millis() - lastPressTime >
debounceDelay)) {
        x += 1.0; // Move 1 unit along the x-axis for each button press
        y += 0.5; // Simulate movement along the y-axis
        distance = sqrt((x * x) + (y * y)); // Calculate distance using
Pythagorean theorem
        int brightness = int((distance / 10.0) * 255); // Scale
distance to 0-255 for LED brightness
        analogWrite(LEDPin, brightness); // Set LED brightness based on
distance
        Serial.print("Distance: ");
        Serial.println(distance); // Print distance on Serial Monitor
        lastPressTime = millis(); // Update last press time
    }
}
```

Code Walkthrough:

- *float x = 0.0;* and *float y = 0.0;* initialize movement along the x and y axes.
- *if (digitalRead(buttonPin) == LOW && (millis() - lastPressTime > debounceDelay))* checks for button press and debounces it using *millis()*.
- *x += 1.0;* simulates movement along the x-axis, and *y += 0.5;* simulates movement along the y-axis.
- *distance = sqrt((x * x) + (y * y));* calculates the distance using the Pythagorean theorem.
- *int brightness = int((distance / 10.0) * 255);* scales the distance to the PWM range (0-255).
- *analogWrite(LEDPin, brightness);* adjusts the LED brightness based on the calculated distance.

- *Serial.println(distance);* prints the calculated distance to the Serial Monitor for real-time monitoring.

Note:
This project demonstrates how to simulate distance calculation using button presses to represent movement along axes. The Pythagorean theorem is used to calculate the distance, which is then displayed either as LED brightness or through the Serial Monitor for easy visualization.

Chapter Summary

In this chapter, we covered essential math functions such as *abs()*, *max()*, *min()*, value mapping with *map()*, power calculations with *pow()*, square root operations using *sqrt()*, rounding functions like *round()*, *ceil()*, and *floor()*, and generating random numbers with *random()*. These functions provide essential mathematical capabilities for creating dynamic and efficient Arduino programs for ESP32/ESP8266 projects.

Chapter-8 Data type conversions

This chapter explains how to convert between different data types in Arduino programming for ESP32/ESP8266. Data type conversions are important for handling different kinds of data, such as sensor values, inputs, and mathematical calculations. We explore conversions like **Float to Integer**, **String to Integer**, **Integer to Float**, **String to Float**, and various other conversions involving **Characters**, **Strings**, and **Booleans**.

Syntax Table

Topics	Syntax	Simple Example
Float to Integer	*(int)floatValue;* or *int(floatValue);*	*float number = 4.9; int intValue = (int)number;*

String to Integer	int value = stringVariable.toInt();	String numberString = "123"; int number = numberString.toInt();
Integer to Float	(float)intVariable; or float(intVariable);	int intValue = 10; float floatValue = (float)intValue;
String to Float	float value = stringVariable.toFloat();	String floatString = "123.45"; float number = floatString.toFloat();
Integer to Character	(char)intVariable;	int asciiCode = 65; char character = (char)asciiCode;
Character to Integer	(int)charVariable;	char character = 'A'; int asciiValue = (int)character;
Integer to String	String stringVariable = String(intVariable);	int number = 123; String numberString = String(number);
Float to String	String stringVariable = String(floatVariable, decimalPlaces);	float temperature = 23.4567; String tempString = String(temperature, 2);
Integer to Boolean	(boolean)intVariable;	int value = 10; boolean boolValue = (boolean)value;
Boolean to Integer	(int)boolVariable;	boolean boolValue = true; int intValue = (int)boolValue;

1. Integer Conversions

Float to Integer:

Converting a float to an integer involves removing the decimal part of the floating-point number, effectively rounding down towards zero. The result is an integer without any fractional component.

Why is Important
This conversion is important when you need to work with whole numbers, especially in tasks that require precise integer values, such as counting items, addressing memory locations, or controlling devices like motors and LEDs where fractional values are unnecessary or unsupported.

Syntax

```
(int)floatValue;
or int(floatValue);
```

Syntax Explanation
To convert a floating-point number to an integer, you can cast the float to an integer using *(int)* or the *int()* function. This operation discards the decimal part and returns only the integer part.

Code Example

```
float number = 4.9;
int intValue = (int)number;
Serial.println(intValue); // Output: 4
```

Notes

- This conversion always rounds towards zero, meaning it truncates the fractional part without rounding up or down.
- This method is useful when the decimal portion is not needed, and you want to work with integer values only.

Warnings

- Be aware that simply casting the float to an integer truncates the decimal part, which might lead to loss of data if precision is important.
- Negative floating-point numbers will also be rounded towards zero, meaning that *-4.9* will become *-4*, not *-5*.

String to Integer:

Converting a string that represents a number into an integer allows you to use numeric operations on values that are initially stored as text. For example, a string like "123" can be converted into the integer 123 for mathematical calculations.

Why is Important
Converting strings to integers is important when dealing with input data in the form of text, such as data received from serial input, sensors, or user inputs, that needs to be processed as a number. It allows you to perform calculations and operations that are not possible with string data types.

Syntax

```
int value = stringVariable.toInt();
```

Syntax Explanation
stringVariable is the string that contains the numeric value. The *toInt()* function converts the string to an integer. If the string doesn't contain a valid number, it will return 0.

Code Example

```
String numberString = "123";
int number = numberString.toInt();
Serial.println(number); // Output: 123
```

Notes

- The *toInt()* function works with the String class in Arduino. It converts valid numeric strings into integers.
- If the string contains non-numeric characters, the conversion may not work as expected, and the result will default to 0 if no valid number is found.

Warnings

- Ensure that the string actually represents a valid number. If the string is empty or contains non-numeric characters, the result will be 0, which may not be the desired outcome.
- Be cautious when converting large numbers from strings, as the resulting integer could overflow if it exceeds the limits of the integer data type on the ESP32/ESP8266.

2. Float Conversions

Integer to Float:

Converting an integer to a float allows you to represent a number with decimal precision. This is useful when you need to perform calculations that require fractions or when working with sensors that provide data with decimal values.

Why is Important
In some applications, you need more precision than integers can provide. By converting an integer to a float, you can introduce decimal precision for more accurate results, especially in calculations involving measurements, sensor data, or time intervals.

Syntax

```
(float)intVariable;
or float(intVariable);
```

Syntax Explanation

intVariable is the integer you want to convert to a float. The casting *(float)* or using *float()* converts the integer into a floating-point number, allowing it to handle decimal places.

Code Example

```
int intValue = 10;
float floatValue = (float)intValue;
Serial.println(floatValue); // Output: 10.00
```

Notes

- Converting an integer to a float enables decimal precision, even though the integer itself does not have any decimal places.
- This is useful when you need to perform calculations that require division or other operations that can result in non-whole numbers.

Warnings

- Be mindful that converting large integers to floats can result in a loss of precision for very large values, due to the limitations of floating-point representation.
- Floats take up more memory than integers, so use them only when necessary to save memory on microcontrollers with limited resources.

String to Float:

Converting a string to a float allows a numeric string, such as "123.45", to be used as a floating-point number. This is useful for performing calculations on data received as text, such as sensor readings or user input.

Why is Important
String to float conversion is important when working with data that is initially in text form (such as serial communication or file inputs) but needs to be processed as a decimal number for accurate calculations. It enables handling numeric values with decimal places for more precise operations.

Syntax

```
float value = stringVariable.toFloat();
```

Syntax Explanation
stringVariable is the string that contains the numeric value in text form. The *toFloat()* function converts the string to a floating-point number (float). If the string does not contain a valid number, it will return 0.0.

Code Example

```
String floatString = "123.45";
float number = floatString.toFloat();
Serial.println(number); // Output: 123.45
```

Notes

- The *toFloat()* function is part of the Arduino String class and can handle both integer and decimal numbers in string form.
- If the string contains non-numeric characters, the result will default to 0.0.

Warnings

- Ensure the string represents a valid numeric format. If the string contains invalid characters or symbols, the conversion may fail, returning 0.0.
- Be cautious with large or very small numbers, as float precision may be limited on microcontrollers like ESP32/ESP8266.

3. Character and String Conversions

Integer to Character:

Converting an integer to a character means taking an ASCII code (a numerical representation of a character) and turning it into its corresponding character. For example, the integer 65 corresponds to the character 'A'.

Why is Important
This conversion is important when you want to manipulate or display characters based on their ASCII codes. It's commonly used in communication protocols, data processing, and displaying text, where you need to handle data in both numerical and character formats.

Syntax

```
char character = (char)intVariable;
```

Syntax Explanation
intVariable is the integer that represents an ASCII code. Casting it to *char* using *(char)* converts the integer to its corresponding ASCII character.

Code Example

```
int asciiCode = 65;
char character = (char)asciiCode;
Serial.println(character); // Output: A
```

Notes
- Each character in the ASCII table has a corresponding numerical value, making it easy to convert between numbers and characters.
- The range of valid ASCII codes is from 0 to 127 for standard characters, but extended ASCII can support up to 255.

Warnings

- Ensure that the integer value is within the valid ASCII range (0-127 for standard characters). Values outside this range may not correspond to printable characters.
- Be cautious when working with non-printable ASCII codes (such as control characters) as they may not display or behave as expected when printed to the serial monitor.

Character to Integer:

Converting a character to its ASCII code means taking a character like 'A' and converting it to its corresponding integer value, such as 65. Each character in the ASCII table has a unique numerical representation.

Why is Important
This conversion is important when you need to process or analyze characters as numerical values. It is especially useful in low-level communication, data encoding, and debugging, where you might need to work with the ASCII codes of characters for transmission or comparison purposes.

Syntax

```
int asciiValue = (int)charVariable;
```

Syntax Explanation
charVariable is the character you want to convert to its ASCII code. Casting it to *int* using *(int)* converts the character into its corresponding integer ASCII value.

Code Example

```
char character = 'A';
int asciiValue = (int)character;
Serial.println(asciiValue); // Output: 65
```

Notes

- Each character in the ASCII table has a numerical code, from 0 to 127 for standard ASCII characters and up to 255 for extended ASCII.
- This conversion is useful for comparing characters or transmitting character data as numbers in protocols that require it.

Warnings

- Ensure you are working with printable characters or standard control characters in the ASCII table. Non-printable ASCII codes (like control characters) may not behave as expected when displayed.
- Be mindful that extended ASCII characters (128-255) might not be supported in all systems or displays.

Integer to String:

Converting an integer to a string allows you to display the numeric value as text, which is useful for printing data to the Serial Monitor, LCDs, or other displays. It enables the handling of numbers in text-based contexts, such as user interfaces or data logging.

Why is Important
This conversion is essential when you need to display or transmit numeric data as a string. It is useful in situations where you want to combine numbers with text or send numbers as part of a message in communication protocols or data logging systems.

Syntax

```
String stringVariable = String(intVariable);
```

Syntax Explanation
intVariable is the integer value you want to convert to a string. The *String()* function converts the integer to its string representation, which can be used for displaying or transmitting.

Code Example

```
int number = 123;
String numberString = String(number);
Serial.println(numberString); // Output: "123"
```

Notes

- The *String()* function simplifies the conversion of numbers to strings, making it easy to display integers as text on various output devices.
- This conversion is particularly useful when combining numeric data with text, such as printing a message with a variable value.

Warnings

- Using the *String()* class can increase memory usage, especially on memory-constrained devices like the ESP8266. Be mindful of how many strings are created to avoid running out of RAM.
- For critical memory-saving tasks, consider using character arrays or alternative methods to handle strings if needed for more efficient memory usage.

Float to String:

Converting a float to a string allows you to represent a floating-point number (with decimal precision) as text. This is useful when you need to display the float value or send it as part of a communication protocol.

Why is Important

This conversion is important when working with sensor data or calculations that produce floating-point numbers, and you need to display or transmit the result in a readable format. It is essential for creating human-readable output or sending data over serial communication or to displays like LCDs.

Syntax

```
String stringVariable = String(floatVariable, decimalPlaces);
```

Syntax Explanation

floatVariable is the floating-point number to be converted to a string. *decimalPlaces* specifies the number of decimal places to include in the string representation. This helps control the precision of the displayed number.

Code Example

```
float temperature = 23.4567;
String tempString = String(temperature, 2);
Serial.println(tempString); // Output: "23.46"
```

Notes

- The *String()* function is a simple way to convert floating-point numbers to strings for display or communication.
- The second argument in the *String()* function controls the number of decimal places, allowing you to format the number for more or less precision.

Warnings

- Be cautious with memory usage when working with *String()* on microcontrollers like the ESP8266, which have limited RAM. Excessive string manipulations can lead to memory fragmentation.
- If precision beyond a few decimal places is not required, it's a good idea to limit the number of decimal places to prevent unnecessary use of memory or transmission bandwidth.

4. Boolean Conversions

Integer to Boolean:

Converting an integer to a boolean means treating the integer as a logical value, where 0 is converted to *false*, and any non-zero value is converted to *true*. This is useful in control structures, logic comparisons, or activating/deactivating states based on numerical conditions.

Why is Important
This conversion is important for simplifying logic in programs. Many sensors and hardware components return numeric values, but in certain conditions, you may only need to check whether a value is zero or non-zero. This allows you to create more readable and efficient code by treating integers as booleans.

Syntax

```
boolean boolVariable = (boolean)intVariable;
```

Syntax Explanation
intVariable is the integer you want to convert. When cast to a *boolean*, 0 becomes *false* and any non-zero value becomes *true*.

Code Example

```
int value = 10;
boolean boolValue = (boolean)value;
if (boolValue) {
Serial.println("True"); // Output: "True"
} else {
Serial.println("False");
}
```

Notes

- The conversion from integer to boolean simplifies decision-making in your program. You don't need to explicitly check if a value is zero or non-zero; simply casting the integer allows for immediate boolean use in conditions.
- This is often used in conditions where the existence of a non-zero value is enough to trigger a logical operation.

Warnings

- Be aware that any non-zero value, whether positive or negative, will be treated as *true*. If you need more specific logic, handle those cases separately.
- This conversion does not modify the integer value itself, but simply interprets it as a boolean for logic purposes.

Boolean to Integer:

Converting a boolean to an integer means translating *false* into *0* and *true* into *1*. This is useful when you need to store boolean values as numbers or send boolean data as numeric values for processing or communication.

Why is Important
This conversion is important when you need to represent boolean logic (true/false) in numeric form. It is commonly used when working with systems or protocols that expect numerical data, such as writing data to memory, transmitting over serial, or logging results.

Syntax

```
int intVariable = (int)boolVariable;
```

Syntax Explanation
boolVariable is the boolean value you want to convert to an integer. When cast to an *int*, *false* becomes *0* and *true* becomes *1*.

Code Example

```
boolean boolValue = true;
int intValue = (int)boolValue;
Serial.println(intValue); // Output: 1
```

Notes

- Converting boolean values to integers allows you to store or transmit boolean states as numerical data.
- This is useful in applications where you want to log or communicate boolean states in a format that requires numbers.

Warnings

- Ensure that the logic of your program does not unintentionally convert other non-boolean values when casting. Always handle boolean-to-integer conversions explicitly to avoid unexpected results.
- Remember that *false* is always *0*, and *true* is always *1*. If you need different numerical representations, you'll need to implement custom logic.

Project- 1. Analog to Digital Value Converter for LED Brightness for Arduino ESP32/ESP8266

Read the analog value from a potentiometer using *analogRead()*, which returns an *int*, then convert the *int* value into a *float* to achieve more precise control over LED brightness. The value is scaled to fit the PWM range using the *map()* function. This project demonstrates how to convert between data types and use the resulting *float* for smooth brightness control.

Requirement:

- ESP32 or ESP8266 board
- LED
- Potentiometer
- Resistor (220Ω for the LED)

Circuit Connection:

1. Connect the potentiometer's middle pin to an analog input pin (e.g., GPIO 34).
2. Connect one side of the potentiometer to 3.3V and the other side to GND.
3. Connect the LED anode (+) to a PWM-capable GPIO pin (e.g., GPIO 2) and the cathode (-) to GND.
4. Add a 220Ω resistor in series with the LED to limit current.

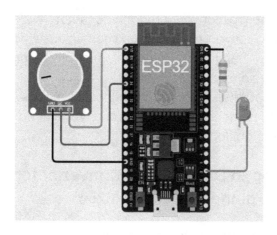

Circuit Analysis:

The analog value from the potentiometer is read using *analogRead()*. This value, an *int* ranging from 0 to 4095, is then converted to a *float* to provide more precise control over LED brightness. The value is scaled to match the PWM range (0-255) using the *map()* function, and the brightness is set using *analogWrite()*.

How it works:

1. The analog value from the potentiometer is read using *analogRead()*.
2. The *int* value is converted to a *float* for more precise brightness control.
3. The value is scaled using the *map()* function to fit the PWM range.
4. The brightness is applied to the LED using *analogWrite()*.

Code:

```
int potPin = 34;
int LEDPin = 2;
int potValue = 0;
float brightness = 0.0;
void setup() {
    pinMode(LEDPin, OUTPUT);
}
void loop() {
    potValue = analogRead(potPin); // Read analog value from
potentiometer
    brightness = map(potValue, 0, 4095, 0, 255); // Scale value to PWM
range
    analogWrite(LEDPin, (int)brightness); // Write scaled value to LED
    delay(10); // Small delay for smoother transition
}
```

Code Walkthrough:

- *int potValue = analogRead(potPin);* reads the analog input from the potentiometer and stores it as an *int* value (0-4095).
- *float brightness = map(potValue, 0, 4095, 0, 255);* scales the potentiometer value from 0-4095 to the PWM range of 0-255 and converts it to a *float*.
- *analogWrite(LEDPin, (int)brightness);* converts the *float* brightness value back to an *int* and writes it to the LED to control its brightness.
- *delay(10);* adds a short delay to create a smooth transition in brightness changes.

Note:

This project demonstrates how to read an analog value from a potentiometer, convert the value from *int* to *float* for better precision, and scale it to control the brightness of an LED using PWM. The *map()* function is used to easily scale the value between the potentiometer range and the PWM range.

2. Temperature Converter (Celsius to Fahrenheit) for Arduino ESP32/ESP8266

Simulate temperature conversion by using a *float* variable to store the temperature in Celsius. Use a *for* loop to increment the temperature value and convert it to Fahrenheit using the standard formula. Convert the resulting *float* Fahrenheit value to an *int* using the *round()* function, and display the rounded temperature on the Serial Monitor.

Requirement:

- ESP32 or ESP8266 board
- Arduino IDE

Circuit Analysis:

The project uses a *for* loop to simulate temperature values in Celsius. Each Celsius value is converted to Fahrenheit using the formula $F = (C * 9/5) + 32$. The Fahrenheit value is a *float*, which is then converted to an *int* using the *round()* function and displayed in the Serial Monitor.

How it works:

1. A *float* variable stores the Celsius temperature.
2. The *for* loop increments the Celsius temperature step by step.
3. At each step, the Celsius temperature is converted to Fahrenheit.
4. The Fahrenheit value is rounded to an *int* and displayed on the Serial Monitor.

Code:

```
float celsius = 0.0;
int fahrenheit = 0;
void setup() {
    Serial.begin(115200);
}
void loop() {
    for (int i = 0; i <= 100; i++) {
        celsius = i;
        float tempFahrenheit = (celsius * 9.0 / 5.0) + 32.0;
        fahrenheit = round(tempFahrenheit);
        Serial.print("Celsius: ");
        Serial.print(celsius);
        Serial.print(" °C, Fahrenheit: ");
        Serial.print(fahrenheit);
        Serial.println(" °F");
        delay(500);
    }
}
```

Code Walkthrough:

- *float celsius = 0.0;* initializes the Celsius temperature as a float.
- *for (int i = 0; i <= 100; i++)* simulates temperature values from 0°C to 100°C.
- *float tempFahrenheit = (celsius * 9.0 / 5.0) + 32.0;* converts the Celsius value to Fahrenheit.
- *fahrenheit = round(tempFahrenheit);* converts the *float* value to an *int* using the *round()* function for accurate display.
- *Serial.print()* outputs both Celsius and Fahrenheit values to the Serial Monitor.
- *delay(500);* adds a delay to ensure the output is easy to read.

Note:

This project demonstrates how to simulate temperature conversion and display the results on the Serial Monitor. The use of a *for* loop, data type conversion, and mathematical functions like *round()* helps beginners understand basic calculations and how to display results in Arduino.

2. String to Integer Converter for LED Blink for Arduino ESP32/ESP8266

Receive user input via the Serial Monitor as a *String*, convert this string to an *int* using the *toInt()* function, and use the resulting integer value to control how fast an LED blinks. For example, if the user enters "500", the LED will blink with a 500 ms delay between on/off states.

Requirement:

- ESP32 or ESP8266 board
- LED
- Resistor (220Ω for the LED)

Circuit Connection:

1. Connect the LED anode (+) to a GPIO pin (e.g., GPIO 2), and the cathode (-) to GND.
2. Add a 220Ω resistor in series with the LED to limit current.

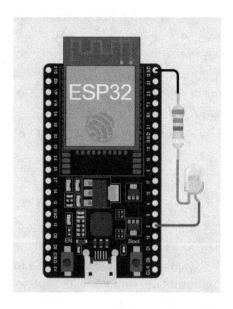

Circuit Analysis:

The project takes a *String* input from the Serial Monitor, converts it to an *int* using the *toInt()* function, and uses this value to control the delay for blinking the LED. The LED blinks at the speed specified by the user input.

How it works:

1. A *String* input is received from the Serial Monitor.
2. The string is converted to an *int* using the *toInt()* function.
3. The resulting integer is used in a *while* loop to control the delay for blinking the LED using *digitalWrite()*.

Code:

```
String inputString = "";
int blinkDelay = 1000;
int LEDPin = 2;
void setup() {
    pinMode(LEDPin, OUTPUT);
    Serial.begin(115200);
}
void loop() {
    if (Serial.available() > 0) {
        inputString = Serial.readString();
        blinkDelay = inputString.toInt();
    }
    digitalWrite(LEDPin, HIGH);
    delay(blinkDelay);
    digitalWrite(LEDPin, LOW);
    delay(blinkDelay);
}
```

Code Walkthrough:

- *String inputString = "";* initializes an empty string to store the user input.
- *Serial.available() > 0* checks if any data has been entered into the Serial Monitor.
- *inputString = Serial.readString();* reads the user input and stores it as a string.
- *blinkDelay = inputString.toInt();* converts the string input into an integer using *toInt()* for controlling the LED blink delay.

- *digitalWrite(LEDPin, HIGH);* and *digitalWrite(LEDPin, LOW);* toggle the LED on and off, while *delay(blinkDelay);* sets the on/off delay based on the converted input.

Note:
This project demonstrates how to take user input from the Serial Monitor, convert it from a *String* to an *int*, and use it to control the blink rate of an LED. It's a simple yet effective way to understand data type conversion and user interaction in Arduino projects.

Chapter Summary

In this chapter, we covered various data type conversions, such as converting *Float to Integer*, *String to Integer*, *Integer to Float*, *String to Float*, *Integer to Character*, and conversions involving *Booleans*. Understanding these conversions helps in efficiently handling different data types in Arduino programming, ensuring flexibility in managing data from inputs, sensors, or user interactions.

Chapter-9 ESP32 Networking (Wi-Fi)

1. Basic Wi-Fi Setup

Connect to a Wi-Fi Network Using the SSID and Password

WiFi.begin(ssid, password) is a function used in Arduino programming for ESP32 and ESP8266 microcontrollers. It allows the device to connect to a Wi-Fi network using the provided network name (SSID) and password.

Why is Important?
Connecting to a Wi-Fi network is crucial for ESP32 and ESP8266 because these microcontrollers are typically used in IoT (Internet of Things) applications that require internet access. This function enables the board to send or receive data over a network, which is essential for creating connected smart devices.

Syntax

```
WiFi.begin(ssid, password);
```

Syntax Explanation

- *ssid*: The name of the Wi-Fi network you want to connect to.
- *password*: The password for the Wi-Fi network.

Code Example

```
WiFi.begin("YourNetworkName", "YourPassword");
```

Notes

- Make sure that the SSID and password are correct, as incorrect details will prevent the device from connecting to the network.
- The connection process may take a few seconds. You may need to include code to check the connection status.

Warnings

- Avoid hard-coding sensitive information like passwords directly in your code. It can pose a security risk if someone gets access to the code.
- Make sure your Wi-Fi credentials are compatible with the Wi-Fi module (e.g., supported encryption type).

Set up the ESP32 as a Wi-Fi Access Point

WiFi.softAP(ssid, password) is a function used in Arduino programming for ESP32 and ESP8266 microcontrollers to set up the device as a Wi-Fi access point (AP). This allows other devices to connect directly to the ESP32 or ESP8266 without needing an external router.

Why is Important?
Setting up an ESP32 or ESP8266 as an access point is useful for creating a private network where other devices can connect directly. This is especially helpful in IoT projects where you may need to control or gather data from multiple devices without relying on an existing Wi-Fi network.

Syntax

```
WiFi.softAP(ssid, password);
```

Syntax Explanation

- *ssid*: The name you want to assign to the Wi-Fi network being created by the ESP32.
- *password*: The password to connect to this network. The password must be at least 8 characters long.

Code Example

```
WiFi.softAP("MyESP32Network", "MyPassword123");
```

Notes

- The ESP32 will create a new Wi-Fi network that other devices can see and connect to using the provided SSID and password.

- This function can be particularly useful in scenarios where a direct point-to-point connection is needed without using an external router.

Warnings

- Ensure that the password is at least 8 characters long, as shorter passwords will not be accepted.
- This network will be open if no password is set, which may be a security risk if you need to restrict access.

Disconnect from the Current Wi-Fi Network

WiFi.disconnect() is a function used in Arduino programming for ESP32 and ESP8266 microcontrollers to disconnect the device from the currently connected Wi-Fi network.

Why is Important?
Disconnecting from a Wi-Fi network is useful when you need to stop communication temporarily or switch to another network. It can help in managing power consumption, debugging connection issues, or ensuring that the device does not attempt to connect to an undesired network.

Syntax

```
WiFi.disconnect();
```

Syntax Explanation

- *WiFi*: The object that controls Wi-Fi operations.
- *disconnect()*: This function will sever the existing connection to the Wi-Fi network.

Code Example

```
WiFi.disconnect();
```

Notes

- After calling WiFi.disconnect(), the ESP32 or ESP8266 will no longer be connected to any network until another connection attempt is made using *WiFi.begin()*.
- It is often used in conjunction with conditional statements to manage multiple Wi-Fi states.

Warnings

- Disconnecting from the network will result in loss of internet connectivity, which may interrupt any ongoing data transmission.
- Use this function carefully if the device is performing a critical operation over Wi-Fi, as it will stop all network activities.

Project- 1: ESP32 Wi-Fi Connection: Connect the ESP32 to Your Home Wi-Fi and Display the Connection Status on the Serial Monitor

Object
To connect the ESP32 microcontroller to your home Wi-Fi network and display the connection status on the serial monitor.

Requirement

- ESP32 development board
- USB cable
- Arduino IDE
- Wi-Fi network credentials (SSID and password)

Circuit Connection

- Connect the ESP32 to your computer using a USB cable. This provides both power and data connectivity.

Circuit Analysis

- The ESP32 will be powered through the USB connection to your computer. The serial monitor will be used to display the status of the Wi-Fi connection. No additional components are needed for this project, making it a simple and straightforward connection.

How to Work

1. The ESP32 will be programmed with Arduino IDE to connect to a Wi-Fi network using the provided SSID and password.
2. The serial monitor will display messages indicating the connection process and whether the connection was successful.
3. Once connected, the ESP32 can be used for various IoT applications, such as controlling devices over Wi-Fi or sending data to a server.

Use Syntax

```
WiFi.begin(ssid, password);
WiFi.status();
```

Code

```
#include <WiFi.h> const char ssid = "YourNetworkName";*
const char password = "YourPassword";*
void setup() { Serial.begin(115200);
WiFi.begin(ssid, password);
Serial.print("Connecting to WiFi...");
while (WiFi.status() != WL_CONNECTED) { delay(1000);
Serial.print(".");
}
Serial.println("Connected!"); Serial.print("IP Address: ");
Serial.println(WiFi.localIP());
}
void loop() { // Do nothing here for now
}
```

Code Walkthrough

- *#include <WiFi.h>*: This library is used for Wi-Fi functionality in ESP32.
- *const char* ssid = "YourNetworkName"; const char* password = "YourPassword";*: These variables store the SSID and password of your Wi-Fi network.
- *Serial.begin(115200);*: Initializes serial communication at a baud rate of 115200 to display messages on the serial monitor.
- *WiFi.begin(ssid, password);*: Attempts to connect to the Wi-Fi network with the given SSID and password.
- *while (WiFi.status() != WL_CONNECTED)*: This loop runs until the ESP32 successfully connects to the Wi-Fi network, printing a dot for each second of delay to indicate connection progress.
- *Serial.println("Connected!");*: Displays a message indicating that the ESP32 is successfully connected to the network.
- *Serial.print("IP Address: "); Serial.println(WiFi.localIP());*: Prints the local IP address assigned to the ESP32.

Note

- Make sure to replace *"YourNetworkName"* and *"YourPassword"* with your actual Wi-Fi credentials.
- The connection process might take some time, depending on the signal strength and other network conditions.

2. Connection Status & IP Information

Check the Wi-Fi Connection Status

WiFi.status() is a function used in Arduino programming for ESP32 and ESP8266 microcontrollers to check the current status of the Wi-Fi connection, such as whether the device is connected to a network or not.

Why is Important?

WiFi.status() is crucial for monitoring the connection state of the ESP32 or ESP8266. It helps in determining if the connection was successful, handling reconnections, or executing specific actions when the device gets disconnected. This is especially important for reliable IoT applications.

Syntax

```
WiFi.status();
```

Syntax Explanation

- *WiFi*: The object used for managing Wi-Fi operations.
- *status()*: Returns the current status of the Wi-Fi connection. The return value is typically a status code like *WL_CONNECTED* if connected or another code representing various states (e.g., no connection, connection failed).

Code Example

```
void loop() {
  if (WiFi.status() == WL_CONNECTED) {
    Serial.println("Wi-Fi is connected!");
  } else if (WiFi.status() == WL_NO_SSID_AVAIL) {
    Serial.println("Wi-Fi SSID not available!");
  } else if (WiFi.status() == WL_CONNECT_FAILED) {
    Serial.println("Wi-Fi connection failed! Check your password.");
  } else if (WiFi.status() == WL_DISCONNECTED) {
    Serial.println("Wi-Fi is disconnected! Attempting
reconnection...");
    WiFi.begin("YourNetworkName", "YourPassword");
  } else {
    Serial.println("Wi-Fi status unknown.");
  }
  delay(1000);
}
```

Notes

- The *WiFi.status()* function can return multiple status codes:
  - *WL_CONNECTED*: The ESP32 is successfully connected to the network.
  - *WL_NO_SSID_AVAIL*: The requested SSID is not available.
  - *WL_CONNECT_FAILED*: The connection failed, possibly due to incorrect credentials.
  - *WL_DISCONNECTED*: The ESP32 is disconnected from the network.
- The return value of *WiFi.status()* can be very useful for debugging and creating stable connections by providing appropriate feedback and responses based on different scenarios.

Warnings

- Relying solely on *WiFi.status()* without implementing reconnection logic may lead to your device staying disconnected indefinitely if it loses the network. Make sure to include recovery strategies for reliable operation.
- When checking *WiFi.status()*, ensure you use proper delay or handling mechanisms to prevent unnecessary busy-waiting, which can block other code from running efficiently.

Get the IP Address of the ESP32 When Connected to Wi-Fi

WiFi.localIP() is a function used in Arduino programming for ESP32 and ESP8266 microcontrollers to retrieve the local IP address assigned to the device when it is successfully connected to a Wi-Fi network.

Why is Important?
The IP address is essential for communication in a network. Knowing the local IP address of the ESP32 allows you to access it from other devices on the same network, enabling tasks like sending

data, controlling the ESP32, or building a web server. This is especially important for IoT projects that require direct interaction with the device.

Syntax

```
WiFi.localIP();
```

Syntax Explanation

- *WiFi*: The object responsible for Wi-Fi operations.
- *localIP()*: Returns the local IP address of the ESP32 in the form of an IPAddress object.

Code Example

```
void setup() {
  Serial.begin(115200);
  WiFi.begin("YourNetworkName", "YourPassword");
  while (WiFi.status() != WL_CONNECTED) {
    delay(1000);
    Serial.print(".");
  }
  Serial.println("Connected to Wi-Fi!");
  Serial.print("ESP32 IP Address: ");
  Serial.println(WiFi.localIP());
}
void loop() {
  // Your main code here
}
```

Notes

- The *WiFi.localIP()* function will return a valid IP address only after the ESP32 has successfully connected to a Wi-Fi network.
- The local IP address is typically assigned by your router, and it can be used to communicate directly with the ESP32 from other devices on the same network.

Warnings

- If the ESP32 is not connected to the network, *WiFi.localIP()* may return *0.0.0.0*, indicating that no valid IP address has been assigned.
- Depending on the router's DHCP configuration, the local IP address assigned to your ESP32 may change each time it reconnects. To ensure a fixed address, consider setting up a static IP configuration.

Get the IP Address of the ESP32 When in Access Point Mode

WiFi.softAPIP() is a function used in Arduino programming for ESP32 and ESP8266 microcontrollers to retrieve the IP address assigned to the ESP32 when it is set up as a Wi-Fi access point (AP). This allows other devices to connect directly to the ESP32 network.

Why is Important?
Knowing the IP address of the ESP32 when it is in Access Point mode is crucial for communication with other devices connected to the network it creates. This is especially useful when building local networks where the ESP32 serves as a host, allowing devices to interact with it directly, such as controlling GPIOs or serving a web page.

Syntax

```
WiFi.softAPIP();
```

Syntax Explanation

- *WiFi*: The object that manages Wi-Fi operations.
- *softAPIP()*: Returns the IP address of the ESP32 when it is in Access Point mode. The return value is typically in the form of an IPAddress object, such as *192.168.4.1*.

Code Example

```
void setup() {
  Serial.begin(115200);
  WiFi.softAP("MyESP32Network", "MyPassword123");
  Serial.println("Access Point started!");
  Serial.print("ESP32 AP IP Address: ");
  Serial.println(WiFi.softAPIP());
}
void loop() {
  // Your main code here
}
```

Notes

- The default IP address for the ESP32 when in Access Point mode is usually *192.168.4.1*. This can be used by other devices to connect to the ESP32 and interact with it.
- This function is particularly helpful when setting up a local server hosted on the ESP32, allowing connected devices to access it through a web browser.

Warnings

- Ensure that the devices connecting to the ESP32 AP know the correct IP address in order to establish communication.
- The IP address of the ESP32 in Access Point mode is usually static, but can be customized if needed using additional configurations. Make sure to handle the IP carefully if you have multiple ESP32s acting as access points, to avoid conflicts.

Project: Display ESP32 IP Address

Object
To connect the ESP32 to a Wi-Fi network and display the device's assigned IP address on the serial monitor or an attached screen.

Requirement

- ESP32 development board
- USB cable
- Arduino IDE
- Wi-Fi network credentials (SSID and password)
- (Optional) OLED or LCD display screen

Circuit Connection

- **Serial Monitor**: Connect the ESP32 to your computer using a USB cable. This will provide both power and communication for displaying the IP address on the serial monitor.
- **Optional OLED/LCD Display**: Connect the screen to the ESP32 if you want to display the IP address on a separate screen. Follow the specific wiring guide for your display (e.g., I2C connections to ESP32 pins).

Circuit Analysis

- The ESP32 will connect to a Wi-Fi network and receive an IP address from the router's DHCP.
- The serial monitor will be used to print this IP address, or it will be displayed on a connected screen. This helps verify that the device is successfully connected to the network.

How to Work

1. The ESP32 will be programmed to connect to the specified Wi-Fi network using *WiFi.begin(ssid, password)*.
2. Once connected, the ESP32 will retrieve its local IP address using *WiFi.localIP()*.
3. The IP address will be displayed either on the serial monitor or on an optional OLED/LCD display.

Use Syntax

```
WiFi.begin(ssid, password);
WiFi.localIP();
```

Code

```
#include <WiFi.h> const char ssid = "YourNetworkName";*
const char password = "YourPassword";*
void setup() {
  Serial.begin(115200);
  WiFi.begin(ssid, password);
  Serial.print("Connecting to Wi-Fi...");
  while (WiFi.status() != WL_CONNECTED) {      delay(1000);
    Serial.print(".");
  }
  Serial.println();
  Serial.println("Connected to Wi-Fi!");
  Serial.print("ESP32 IP Address: ");
  Serial.println(WiFi.localIP());
}
void loop() {
  // Your main code here
}
```

Code Walkthrough

- *#include <WiFi.h>*: This library is included to use Wi-Fi functions with ESP32.
- *const char* ssid = "YourNetworkName"; const char* password = "YourPassword";*: These are the Wi-Fi credentials used to connect the ESP32 to your network. Replace with your network's actual SSID and password.
- *Serial.begin(115200);*: Initializes the serial communication to display output on the serial monitor.
- *WiFi.begin(ssid, password);*: Starts the process of connecting the ESP32 to the Wi-Fi network using the specified SSID and password.
- *while (WiFi.status() != WL_CONNECTED)*: This loop keeps running until the ESP32 successfully connects to the Wi-Fi network. It prints a dot every second to indicate progress.
- *Serial.println("Connected to Wi-Fi!");*: Prints a message once the ESP32 is successfully connected.
- *Serial.print("ESP32 IP Address: "); Serial.println(WiFi.localIP());*: Prints the local IP address assigned to the ESP32.

Note

- Replace *"YourNetworkName"* and *"YourPassword"* with the actual SSID and password of your Wi-Fi network.
- Ensure the serial monitor baud rate matches the one used in *Serial.begin(115200)* for correct output display.
- If using an OLED or LCD, you may need to include additional libraries (like *Adafruit_SSD1306.h*) and modify the code to display the IP address on the screen.

3. Wi-Fi Mode Selection

Set the ESP32 to Station Mode (Connect to a Wi-Fi Network)

WiFi.mode(WIFI_STA) is a function used in Arduino programming for ESP32 and ESP8266 microcontrollers to set the device into "Station mode" (STA mode). In this mode, the ESP32 can connect to an existing Wi-Fi network, similar to how a smartphone or laptop connects to a Wi-Fi network.

Why is Important?
Station mode is one of the most common modes for ESP32 in IoT applications because it allows the device to join an existing network, enabling internet access, communication with other devices, or interaction with servers. This mode is essential for scenarios where the ESP32 needs to send data over the internet or be part of a local network.

Syntax

```
WiFi.mode(WIFI_STA);
```

Syntax Explanation

- *WiFi*: The object managing Wi-Fi operations.
- *mode()*: Sets the mode of operation for the Wi-Fi.

- *WIFI_STA*: This parameter indicates "Station mode," meaning the ESP32 will act as a client and connect to an external Wi-Fi network.

Code Example

```
void setup() {
  Serial.begin(115200);
  WiFi.mode(WIFI_STA);
  WiFi.begin("YourNetworkName", "YourPassword");
  while (WiFi.status() != WL_CONNECTED) {
    delay(1000);
    Serial.print(".");
  }
  Serial.println();
  Serial.println("Connected to Wi-Fi in Station mode!");
  Serial.print("IP Address: ");
  Serial.println(WiFi.localIP());
}
void loop() {
  // Your main code here
}
```

Notes

- Station mode is ideal when the ESP32 needs to interact with other networked devices, such as a server or other IoT devices.
- Using *WiFi.mode(WIFI_STA)* ensures that the ESP32 will only try to connect as a client, which helps save power compared to other modes that provide both access point and station functionality.

Warnings

- Setting the ESP32 in station mode alone means it cannot create its own network. If you need the ESP32 to provide a Wi-Fi network for other devices, use *WIFI_AP* or *WIFI_AP_STA* mode instead.
- Make sure to set the Wi-Fi mode before calling *WiFi.begin()*, as the mode defines the type of connection the ESP32 will establish.

Set the ESP32 to Access Point Mode (Create a Wi-Fi Hotspot)

WiFi.mode(WIFI_AP) is a function used in Arduino programming for ESP32 and ESP8266 microcontrollers to set the device into "Access Point mode" (AP mode). In this mode, the ESP32 creates a Wi-Fi network that other devices can connect to, effectively making the ESP32 act as a hotspot.

Why is Important?

Access Point mode is important for creating a local network where multiple devices can connect directly to the ESP32 without needing an external router. This is especially useful for scenarios where you want to control the ESP32 or exchange data with multiple devices in a private, isolated environment, such as in local automation projects or setting up direct communication with smartphones or other IoT devices.

Syntax

```
WiFi.mode(WIFI_AP);
```

Syntax Explanation

- *WiFi*: The object used for managing Wi-Fi operations.
- *mode()*: Sets the mode of operation for the Wi-Fi.
- *WIFI_AP*: This parameter configures the ESP32 to function in Access Point mode, allowing it to create a Wi-Fi hotspot.

Code Example

```
void setup() {
  Serial.begin(115200);
  WiFi.mode(WIFI_AP);
  WiFi.softAP("MyESP32Hotspot", "MyPassword123");
  Serial.println("Access Point created!");
  Serial.print("AP IP Address: ");
  Serial.println(WiFi.softAPIP());
}
void loop() {
  // Your main code here
}
```

Notes

- The default IP address for the ESP32 in Access Point mode is usually *192.168.4.1*. This address can be used by devices to connect to the ESP32 and communicate directly with it.
- The *WiFi.softAP(ssid, password)* function is used to set up the network with a specified SSID and password, allowing for secure access.

Warnings

- In Access Point mode, the ESP32 will not have internet access, and it only acts as a local hotspot. It can handle a limited number of client connections, depending on the memory available.
- Make sure that the password is at least 8 characters long; otherwise, the Access Point setup will fail due to insufficient security measures.

Enable Both Station and Access Point Modes

WiFi.mode(WIFI_AP_STA) is a function used in Arduino programming for ESP32 and ESP8266 microcontrollers to enable both "Station mode" (STA) and "Access Point mode" (AP) simultaneously. This allows the ESP32 to connect to an existing Wi-Fi network while also creating its own hotspot.

Why is Important?
Using both Station and Access Point modes is beneficial in scenarios where you want the ESP32 to interact with an existing network (e.g., accessing the internet or communicating with other devices) while also allowing direct connections from nearby devices. This combination mode is useful for setting up a network gateway, troubleshooting, or providing local access and control to other users.

Syntax

```
WiFi.mode(WIFI_AP_STA);
```

Syntax Explanation

- *WiFi*: The object used for managing Wi-Fi operations.
- *mode()*: Sets the mode of operation for the Wi-Fi.
- *WIFI_AP_STA*: Configures the ESP32 to operate in both Station mode and Access Point mode simultaneously.

Code Example

```
void setup() {
  Serial.begin(115200);
  WiFi.mode(WIFI_AP_STA);
  WiFi.begin("YourNetworkName", "YourPassword");
  while (WiFi.status() != WL_CONNECTED) {
    delay(1000);
    Serial.print(".");
  }
  Serial.println();
  Serial.println("Connected to Wi-Fi as Station!");
  WiFi.softAP("MyESP32Hotspot", "MyPassword123");
  Serial.println("Access Point created!");
  Serial.print("AP IP Address: ");
  Serial.println(WiFi.softAPIP());
  Serial.print("Station IP Address: ");
  Serial.println(WiFi.localIP());
}
void loop() {
  // Your main code here
}
```

Notes

- In *WIFI_AP_STA* mode, the ESP32 acts as both a client and a server. It can connect to an existing Wi-Fi network while also allowing other devices to connect directly to it.
- This mode is especially useful for updating device configurations, where the ESP32 can provide a local access point even when connected to another network.

Warnings

- Running the ESP32 in both Access Point and Station modes simultaneously can consume more power and memory, potentially affecting performance. Ensure that your application can handle these resource requirements.

- The IP address for Access Point mode (*WiFi.softAPIP()*) and Station mode (*WiFi.localIP()*) will be different, and each address serves different functions.

Project: Dual Mode ESP32

Object

To configure the ESP32 to operate in both Station (STA) and Access Point (AP) modes simultaneously. This will allow the ESP32 to connect to an existing Wi-Fi network as a client while also providing its own hotspot for other devices to connect to.

Requirement

- ESP32 development board
- USB cable
- Arduino IDE
- Wi-Fi network credentials (SSID and password)
- (Optional) OLED or LCD display to show connection status

Circuit Connection

- **Serial Monitor**: Connect the ESP32 to your computer using a USB cable to provide both power and enable communication for displaying information on the serial monitor.
- **Optional OLED/LCD Display**: If you want to display the connection status on a separate screen, connect the display to the ESP32 according to the screen's wiring guide (e.g., I2C pins for an OLED).

Circuit Analysis

- The ESP32 will function both as a client connected to a Wi-Fi network and as an access point creating its own network.

- The serial monitor will be used to display the IP addresses for both modes, verifying that the ESP32 is successfully operating in dual mode.

How to Work

1. The ESP32 is programmed to set its Wi-Fi mode to *WIFI_AP_STA*, enabling both Station and Access Point functionality.
2. The *WiFi.begin(ssid, password)* function is used to connect to an existing Wi-Fi network.
3. The *WiFi.softAP(ssid, password)* function creates an AP network for other devices to connect to.
4. Both the Station and AP IP addresses are retrieved and displayed on the serial monitor.

Use Syntax

```
WiFi.mode(WIFI_AP_STA);
WiFi.begin(ssid, password);
WiFi.softAP(ap_ssid, ap_password);
WiFi.localIP();
WiFi.softAPIP();
```

Code

```
#include <WiFi.h>
const char ssid = "YourNetworkName";*
const char password = "YourPassword";*
const char ap_ssid = "ESP32Hotspot";*
const char ap_password = "HotspotPassword";*
void setup() {
  Serial.begin(115200);
  WiFi.mode(WIFI_AP_STA);
  WiFi.begin(ssid, password);
  Serial.print("Connecting to Wi-Fi as Station...");
  while (WiFi.status() != WL_CONNECTED) {
    delay(1000);
    Serial.print(".");
  }
  Serial.println();
  Serial.println("Connected to Wi-Fi as Station!");
  Serial.print("Station IP Address: ");
  Serial.println(WiFi.localIP());
  WiFi.softAP(ap_ssid, ap_password);
  Serial.println("Access Point created!");
  Serial.print("AP IP Address: ");
  Serial.println(WiFi.softAPIP());
```

```
}
void loop() {
  // Your main code here
}
```

Code Walkthrough

- *#include <WiFi.h>*: Includes the Wi-Fi library required for using Wi-Fi functions with ESP32.
- *const char ssid = "YourNetworkName"; const char* password = "YourPassword";**: Stores the credentials for the Wi-Fi network the ESP32 will connect to as a client.
- *const char ap_ssid = "ESP32Hotspot"; const char* ap_password = "HotspotPassword";**: Stores the credentials for the AP network created by the ESP32.
- *WiFi.mode(WIFI_AP_STA);*: Configures the ESP32 to work in both Station and Access Point modes.
- *WiFi.begin(ssid, password);*: Connects the ESP32 to an existing Wi-Fi network.
- *while (WiFi.status() != WL_CONNECTED)*: Keeps running until the ESP32 connects successfully to the Wi-Fi network, printing progress to the serial monitor.
- *WiFi.softAP(ap_ssid, ap_password);*: Sets up the Access Point network with the provided SSID and password.
- *WiFi.localIP()* and *WiFi.softAPIP()*: These functions display the IP addresses for Station mode and Access Point mode, respectively.

Note

- Replace *"YourNetworkName"* and *"YourPassword"* with the credentials of your existing Wi-Fi network, and *"ESP32Hotspot"* and *"HotspotPassword"* with the desired SSID and password for the hotspot.
- This dual mode setup allows the ESP32 to be both connected to your network and provide connectivity for other devices, which is useful for testing, local server access, or bridging different devices in a network.

4. Network Scanning

Scan for Nearby Wi-Fi Networks

WiFi.scanNetworks() is a function used in Arduino programming for ESP32 and ESP8266 microcontrollers to scan for available Wi-Fi networks in the vicinity. It provides details such as SSID, signal strength, and encryption type of nearby networks.

Why is Important?
Scanning nearby networks is useful for selecting the strongest or most suitable network to connect to. It also helps in determining available networks for user configuration, troubleshooting, or logging available networks in an IoT environment.

Syntax

```
WiFi.scanNetworks();
```

Syntax Explanation
- *WiFi*: The object responsible for Wi-Fi operations.
- *scanNetworks()*: This function scans for all available Wi-Fi networks and returns the number of networks detected.

Code Example

```
void setup() {
  Serial.begin(115200);
  Serial.println("Scanning for Wi-Fi networks...");
  int numNetworks = WiFi.scanNetworks();
  for (int i = 0; i < numNetworks; i++) {
    Serial.print("Network name (SSID): ");
    Serial.println(WiFi.SSID(i));
    Serial.print("Signal strength (RSSI): ");
    Serial.println(WiFi.RSSI(i));
    Serial.print("Encryption type: ");
    Serial.println(WiFi.encryptionType(i));
    Serial.println("----------------------");
  }
}
```

```
void loop() {
  // Your main code here
}
```

Notes

- The *WiFi.scanNetworks()* function can be used to provide users with an option to select the Wi-Fi network they want the ESP32 to connect to.
- Scanning networks takes a bit of time (a few seconds), and you might experience delays if you call this function frequently.

Warnings

- Scanning for networks repeatedly can consume significant power and may interfere with ongoing Wi-Fi operations. Use it sparingly in battery-powered applications.
- Ensure that the scan results are not blocking other important tasks in your program. Consider using non-blocking techniques or placing it in an appropriate part of your code, such as during initialization.

Get the SSID of the i-th Network Found in a Scan

WiFi.SSID(i) is a function used in Arduino programming for ESP32 and ESP8266 microcontrollers to retrieve the SSID (name) of a specific Wi-Fi network found during a network scan. The function returns the SSID of the *i-th* network from the list of detected networks.

Why is Important?
Getting the SSID of networks found in a scan is important for displaying available Wi-Fi networks to the user or for selecting a specific network to connect to based on its name. It helps in choosing the correct network when there are multiple networks available.

Syntax

```
WiFi.SSID(i);
```

Syntax Explanation

- *WiFi*: The object that manages Wi-Fi operations.
- *SSID(i)*: Retrieves the SSID of the network found at index *i* from the list of scanned networks. The index *i* should be between 0 and the number of networks found minus one.

Code Example

```
void setup() {
  Serial.begin(115200);
  Serial.println("Scanning for Wi-Fi networks...");
  int numNetworks = WiFi.scanNetworks();
  for (int i = 0; i < numNetworks; i++) {
    Serial.print("Network name (SSID) of network ");
    Serial.print(i + 1);
    Serial.print(": ");
    Serial.println(WiFi.SSID(i));
  }
}
void loop() {
  // Your main code here
}
```

Notes

- The *WiFi.SSID(i)* function should be called after a successful *WiFi.scanNetworks()* to ensure you have a list of available networks.
- The value of *i* must be within the range of networks found. You can use *WiFi.scanNetworks()* to determine the number of available networks before accessing them.

Warnings

- If *i* is out of range (i.e., greater than or equal to the number of networks found), the function may return an empty or undefined value. Ensure you properly check the number of networks detected.

- The SSID may sometimes be hidden, and in such cases, the function may return an empty string, indicating that the network name is not broadcast.

Get the Signal Strength (RSSI) of the i-th Network Found in a Scan

WiFi.RSSI(i) is a function used in Arduino programming for ESP32 and ESP8266 microcontrollers to get the Received Signal Strength Indicator (RSSI) of a specific Wi-Fi network found during a network scan. RSSI is a measure of the power level received by the antenna and is used to determine signal strength.

Why is Important?
The signal strength (RSSI) is important to decide which Wi-Fi network provides the best connection quality. This can help in choosing the network with the strongest signal, especially when there are multiple available networks with the same SSID. Stronger signals generally mean better connectivity and more reliable communication.

Syntax
```
WiFi.RSSI(i);
```

Syntax Explanation

- *WiFi*: The object responsible for Wi-Fi operations.
- *RSSI(i)*: Retrieves the signal strength (in dBm) of the network found at index *i*. The value of RSSI is typically negative, where values closer to 0 indicate a stronger signal.

Code Example
```
void setup() {
  Serial.begin(115200);
  Serial.println("Scanning for Wi-Fi networks...");
  int numNetworks = WiFi.scanNetworks();
  for (int i = 0; i < numNetworks; i++) {
    Serial.print("Network name (SSID) of network ");
    Serial.print(i + 1);
    Serial.print(": ");
    Serial.println(WiFi.SSID(i));
    Serial.print("Signal strength (RSSI): ");
    Serial.println(WiFi.RSSI(i));
    Serial.println("-----------------------");
```

```
  }
}
void loop() {
  // Your main code here
}
```

Notes

- RSSI values are usually negative, and closer to zero indicates a stronger signal (e.g., *-30 dBm* is a strong signal, while *-90 dBm* is weak).
- RSSI helps in determining the best network to connect to, particularly in scenarios where multiple networks are available and you want to select the one with the highest signal strength.

Warnings

- Signal strength can vary depending on physical obstructions, distance, and interference. It is recommended to measure RSSI over multiple readings for more accurate assessment.
- Avoid using only RSSI as the deciding factor for connecting to a network. Other factors, such as security type and network stability, should also be considered for optimal performance.

Project: Wi-Fi Network Scanner

Object
To program the ESP32 to scan for available Wi-Fi networks and display the SSID and signal strength (RSSI) of each detected network.

Requirement

- ESP32 development board
- USB cable
- Arduino IDE

Circuit Connection

- **Serial Monitor**: Connect the ESP32 to your computer using a USB cable. This will provide both power and allow you to view the network scan results on the serial monitor.

Circuit Analysis

- The ESP32 will act as a Wi-Fi scanner, detecting and listing all nearby Wi-Fi networks.
- The detected networks will be displayed on the serial monitor, showing the SSID and signal strength for each network. This provides a clear view of the available networks and their signal quality.

How to Work

1. The ESP32 will be programmed to perform a Wi-Fi scan using *WiFi.scanNetworks()*.
2. For each network found, the SSID and signal strength (RSSI) will be printed on the serial monitor.
3. This allows you to assess which networks are available and determine which one has the best signal quality for connection.

Use Syntax

```
WiFi.scanNetworks();
WiFi.SSID(i);
WiFi.RSSI(i);
```

Code

```
#include <WiFi.h>
void setup() {
  Serial.begin(115200);
  Serial.println("Scanning for Wi-Fi networks...");
  int numNetworks = WiFi.scanNetworks();
  for (int i = 0; i < numNetworks; i++) {
    Serial.print("Network name (SSID) of network ");
    Serial.print(i + 1);
    Serial.print(": ");
    Serial.println(WiFi.SSID(i));
    Serial.print("Signal strength (RSSI): ");
    Serial.println(WiFi.RSSI(i));
    Serial.println("---------------------");
```

```
  }
}
void loop() {
  // Your main code here
}
```

Code Walkthrough

- *#include <WiFi.h>*: Includes the Wi-Fi library necessary for using Wi-Fi functions on the ESP32.
- *Serial.begin(115200);*: Starts the serial communication at a baud rate of 115200 to display output on the serial monitor.
- *WiFi.scanNetworks();*: Performs a scan to detect all available Wi-Fi networks in the vicinity and returns the number of networks found.
- *for (int i = 0; i < numNetworks; i++)*: Loops through each of the networks found to print details.
- *WiFi.SSID(i)*: Retrieves and prints the SSID (name) of the network at index *i*.
- *WiFi.RSSI(i)*: Retrieves and prints the signal strength (RSSI) of the network at index *i*. This value is typically negative, indicating the signal strength in dBm.
- The serial monitor will display the SSID, signal strength, and separator lines for each network.

Note

- Ensure you open the serial monitor at the correct baud rate (*115200*) to see the results properly.
- The signal strength (RSSI) can vary due to interference or obstacles between the ESP32 and the Wi-Fi routers. Multiple scans may give a better estimate of the network environment.
- This project is useful to determine which network provides the best signal, especially when multiple networks are available with the same name.

5. Event Handling

Register a Function to Handle Wi-Fi-Related Events

WiFi.onEvent(WiFiEvent) is a function used in Arduino programming for ESP32 and ESP8266 microcontrollers to register a callback function that handles various Wi-Fi-related events, such as connection, disconnection, or IP address assignment. This function allows you to take specific actions when particular Wi-Fi events occur.

Why is Important?
Handling Wi-Fi events is crucial for monitoring the connection status and taking appropriate actions based on the network state. For example, reconnecting when disconnected or notifying the user of a connection change. This makes your application more robust and capable of recovering from connection issues automatically.

Syntax

```
WiFi.onEvent(WiFiEvent);
```

Syntax Explanation

- *WiFi*: The object responsible for Wi-Fi operations.
- *onEvent(WiFiEvent)*: Registers a callback function (*WiFiEvent*) that will be called when certain Wi-Fi events occur, such as when the ESP32 connects to or disconnects from a Wi-Fi network.

Code Example

```cpp
#include <WiFi.h>
void WiFiEvent(WiFiEvent_t event) {
  switch (event) {
    case SYSTEM_EVENT_STA_CONNECTED:
      Serial.println("Wi-Fi connected!");
      break;
    case SYSTEM_EVENT_STA_DISCONNECTED:
      Serial.println("Wi-Fi disconnected! Attempting reconnection...");
      WiFi.begin("YourNetworkName", "YourPassword");
      break;
    case SYSTEM_EVENT_STA_GOT_IP:
      Serial.print("IP Address: ");
      Serial.println(WiFi.localIP());
      break;
  }
}
void setup() {
  Serial.begin(115200);
  WiFi.onEvent(WiFiEvent);
  WiFi.begin("YourNetworkName", "YourPassword");
  Serial.println("Connecting to Wi-Fi...");
}
void loop() {
  // Your main code here
}
```

Notes

- The *WiFiEvent* function must be defined before *WiFi.onEvent()* to properly handle the Wi-Fi events.
- Handling events like *SYSTEM_EVENT_STA_DISCONNECTED* allows the ESP32 to automatically attempt reconnection, improving network reliability in real-world applications.

Warnings

- Ensure you have all possible events handled properly in the callback to avoid unexpected behaviors.
- Overuse of reconnection attempts can lead to network congestion or connection issues. Set a reasonable delay or limit retries to prevent constant reconnections in case of persistent issues.

Project: Wi-Fi Connection Status Logger

Object

To set up the ESP32 to monitor and log Wi-Fi connection or disconnection events, using *WiFi.onEvent()*, and display the results on the serial monitor.

Requirement

- ESP32 development board
- USB cable
- Arduino IDE

Circuit Connection

- **Serial Monitor**: Connect the ESP32 to your computer using a USB cable. This provides both power and allows you to view logged events on the serial monitor.

Circuit Analysis

- The ESP32 will connect to a Wi-Fi network, and events such as connection, disconnection, and IP assignment will be logged to the serial monitor.
- This allows real-time tracking of the Wi-Fi status, which is useful for monitoring network stability or debugging connectivity issues.

How to Work

1. Use *WiFi.onEvent()* to register a function that will handle Wi-Fi-related events.
2. Define the *WiFiEvent* function to log messages whenever the ESP32 connects, disconnects, or gets an IP address.
3. Connect to a Wi-Fi network using *WiFi.begin()*.
4. Log messages will be displayed on the serial monitor based on the events triggered during the connection process.

Use Syntax

```
WiFi.onEvent(WiFiEvent);
WiFi.begin(ssid, password);
```

Code

```
#include <WiFi.h>
const char ssid = "YourNetworkName";*
const char password = "YourPassword";*
void WiFiEvent(WiFiEvent_t event) {
  switch (event) {
    case SYSTEM_EVENT_STA_CONNECTED:
      Serial.println("Wi-Fi connected!");
      break;
    case SYSTEM_EVENT_STA_DISCONNECTED:
      Serial.println("Wi-Fi disconnected! Attempting reconnection...");
      WiFi.begin(ssid, password);
      break;
    case SYSTEM_EVENT_STA_GOT_IP:
      Serial.print("IP Address assigned: ");
      Serial.println(WiFi.localIP());
      break;
  }
}
void setup() {
  Serial.begin(115200);
  WiFi.onEvent(WiFiEvent);
  WiFi.begin(ssid, password);
  Serial.println("Connecting to Wi-Fi...");
}
void loop() {
  // Your main code here
}
```

Code Walkthrough

- *#include <WiFi.h>*: Includes the Wi-Fi library required for managing Wi-Fi operations.
- *const char* ssid = "YourNetworkName"; const char* password = "YourPassword";*: Stores the credentials needed to connect to your Wi-Fi network.
- *void WiFiEvent(WiFiEvent_t event)*: This function is the event handler that logs Wi-Fi events. It handles *connected*, *disconnected*, and *got IP address* events.

- o *SYSTEM_EVENT_STA_CONNECTED*: Logs when the ESP32 successfully connects to the network.
  - o *SYSTEM_EVENT_STA_DISCONNECTED*: Logs when the ESP32 disconnects from the network and attempts reconnection.
  - o *SYSTEM_EVENT_STA_GOT_IP*: Logs the assigned IP address after successful connection.
- *WiFi.onEvent(WiFiEvent);*: Registers the event handler function to manage Wi-Fi events.
- *WiFi.begin(ssid, password);*: Initiates the connection to the specified Wi-Fi network.
- The *Serial Monitor* will be used to view real-time logs for each Wi-Fi event, allowing users to understand the current state of the connection.

Note

- Replace *"YourNetworkName"* and *"YourPassword"* with your actual Wi-Fi network credentials.
- This setup is useful for debugging Wi-Fi issues or monitoring network stability, as it allows you to see exactly when the device connects, disconnects, or successfully obtains an IP address.
- In case of frequent disconnections, consider adding a delay or limit reconnection attempts to avoid overloading the network or device.

6. Advanced Network Management

Set a Static IP Address, Gateway, and Subnet

WiFi.config(ip, gateway, subnet) is a function used in Arduino programming for ESP32 and ESP8266 microcontrollers to assign a static IP address, along with a specific gateway and subnet mask, to the device. This is done instead of using the default dynamic IP address assigned by the router's DHCP.

Why is Important?

Setting a static IP address is crucial in scenarios where consistent network identification of the ESP32 is needed, such as in home automation systems or network servers. A static IP ensures that the ESP32 always has the same address, making it easier to connect to or control remotely without worrying about the IP address changing over time.

Syntax

```
WiFi.config(ip, gateway, subnet);
```

Syntax Explanation

- *ip*: The static IP address you want to assign to the ESP32 (e.g., *IPAddress(192, 168, 1, 100)*).
- *gateway*: The IP address of the network gateway (typically the router), which is required for external communication (e.g., *IPAddress(192, 168, 1, 1)*).
- *subnet*: The subnet mask for the network, which helps determine the network and host portions of the address (e.g., *IPAddress(255, 255, 255, 0)*).

Code Example

```
#include <WiFi.h>
const char ssid = "YourNetworkName";*
const char password = "YourPassword";*
IPAddress local_IP(192, 168, 1, 184);
IPAddress gateway(192, 168, 1, 1);
IPAddress subnet(255, 255, 255, 0);
void setup() {
  Serial.begin(115200);
  if (!WiFi.config(local_IP, gateway, subnet)) {
    Serial.println("Static IP Configuration Failed");
  } else {
    Serial.println("Static IP Configuration Successful");
  }
  WiFi.begin(ssid, password);
  Serial.println("Connecting to Wi-Fi...");
  while (WiFi.status() != WL_CONNECTED) {
    delay(1000);
```

```
   Serial.print(".");
  }
  Serial.println();
  Serial.print("Connected with IP: ");
  Serial.println(WiFi.localIP());
}
void loop() {
  // Your main code here
}
```

Notes

- Using a static IP address makes it easier to access the ESP32 on the network without worrying about changes in the IP assignment.
- Ensure that the chosen static IP address is not in use by another device and is outside the range of the DHCP server to avoid IP conflicts.

Warnings

- Incorrect configuration of the IP address, gateway, or subnet mask may result in the ESP32 being unable to connect to the network. Make sure to provide valid values that match your network's setup.
- Static IP addresses need to be managed properly to avoid conflicts, which could cause network issues or prevent the ESP32 from accessing the network properly.

Set a Custom Hostname for the ESP32

WiFi.setHostname(name) is a function used in Arduino programming for ESP32 and ESP8266 microcontrollers to assign a custom hostname to the device. This hostname is how the device is identified on the local network instead of using the default name.

Why is Important?
Setting a custom hostname is helpful for easily identifying the ESP32 on a network, especially if multiple devices are connected. Instead of seeing generic names, you can assign meaningful names like "LivingRoomSensor" or "ESP32_Garage" for easier

management and identification when accessing the device or using
network services like DHCP or DNS.

Syntax

```
WiFi.setHostname(name);
```

Syntax Explanation

- *name*: The custom hostname you want to assign to the
  ESP32. It must be a string and should be unique within the
  local network (e.g., *"MyESP32Device"*).

Code Example

```
#include <WiFi.h>
const char ssid = "YourNetworkName";*
const char password = "YourPassword";*
void setup() {
  Serial.begin(115200);
  WiFi.setHostname("CustomESP32");
  WiFi.begin(ssid, password);
  Serial.println("Connecting to Wi-Fi...");
  while (WiFi.status() != WL_CONNECTED) {
    delay(1000);
    Serial.print(".");
  }
  Serial.println();
  Serial.print("Connected! Hostname: ");
  Serial.println(WiFi.getHostname());
  Serial.print("IP Address: ");
  Serial.println(WiFi.localIP());
}
void loop() {
  // Your main code here
}
```

Notes

- The hostname must be set before calling *WiFi.begin()*, as it is applied during the connection process.
- Setting a unique hostname is particularly useful in environments where there are many ESP32 devices, to easily differentiate them without relying on IP addresses.

Warnings

- If the hostname is not unique on the local network, it could cause conflicts that may prevent proper communication between devices.
- Some routers might not fully support custom hostnames or may still display the ESP32 with its default name. Check your router settings if you do not see the expected hostname.

Adjust the Wi-Fi Transmission Power

WiFi.setTxPower(power) is a function used in Arduino programming for ESP32 and ESP8266 microcontrollers to set the transmission power level of the Wi-Fi radio. This allows you to control how far the Wi-Fi signal from the ESP32 can reach.

Why is Important?
Adjusting the transmission power is important for optimizing power consumption and signal strength. Increasing the power helps improve range and connection reliability, while reducing the power can save energy and reduce interference in environments where long-range communication is not required. This is especially useful for battery-powered IoT devices.

Syntax

```
WiFi.setTxPower(power);
```

Syntax Explanation

- *power*: The transmission power level, represented by constants such as:
    - *WIFI_POWER_MINUS_1dBm*
    - *WIFI_POWER_2dBm*
    - *WIFI_POWER_7dBm*
    - *WIFI_POWER_11dBm*
    - *WIFI_POWER_15dBm*
    - *WIFI_POWER_19_5dBm* (maximum power)

Code Example

```
#include <WiFi.h>
void setup() {
  Serial.begin(115200);
  WiFi.begin("YourNetworkName", "YourPassword");
  Serial.println("Connecting to Wi-Fi...");
  while (WiFi.status() != WL_CONNECTED) {
    delay(1000);
    Serial.print(".");
  }
  Serial.println();
  Serial.println("Connected!");
  WiFi.setTxPower(WIFI_POWER_11dBm);
  Serial.println("Wi-Fi transmission power set to 11 dBm.");
}
void loop() {
  // Your main code here
}
```

Notes

- The transmission power should be adjusted based on the specific application. Higher power settings increase range but consume more energy.
- For indoor or short-range applications, reducing the power may help to avoid unnecessary energy consumption and minimize interference with other nearby devices.

Warnings

- Setting the power too low may lead to weak signals, resulting in unreliable communication and frequent disconnections.

- Always ensure that the selected power setting is in compliance with local regulatory requirements, as transmission power limits vary between regions.

Disable Wi-Fi Sleep Mode for Continuous Connection

WiFi.setSleep(false) is a function used in Arduino programming for ESP32 and ESP8266 microcontrollers to disable Wi-Fi sleep mode, ensuring a continuous Wi-Fi connection. By default, the ESP32 may enter a sleep mode to conserve power, which can intermittently disconnect the Wi-Fi connection.

Why is Important?
Disabling Wi-Fi sleep mode is important in applications that require a stable and continuous Wi-Fi connection without interruptions, such as real-time monitoring, video streaming, or online data transmission. It helps ensure that there are no disconnections due to power-saving mechanisms, which can be critical for certain use cases.

Syntax

```
WiFi.setSleep(false);
```

Syntax Explanation

- *WiFi*: The object that controls Wi-Fi operations.
- *setSleep(false)*: Disables Wi-Fi sleep mode to maintain a continuous connection. To enable sleep mode, you would use *WiFi.setSleep(true)*.

Code Example

```
#include <WiFi.h>
const char ssid = "YourNetworkName";*
const char password = "YourPassword";*
void setup() {
  Serial.begin(115200);
  WiFi.setSleep(false);
  WiFi.begin(ssid, password);
  Serial.println("Connecting to Wi-Fi...");
  while (WiFi.status() != WL_CONNECTED) {
    delay(1000);
    Serial.print(".");
  }
  Serial.println();
  Serial.println("Connected! Wi-Fi sleep mode disabled.");
}
void loop() {
  // Your main code here
}
```

Notes

- Disabling sleep mode will increase power consumption, which may be unsuitable for battery-powered devices.
- Use this setting in scenarios where a continuous connection is crucial, such as remote monitoring or devices that need to be always available on the network.

Warnings

- Disabling sleep mode may significantly reduce battery life for portable or battery-powered ESP32 projects.
- Keep in mind that continuous Wi-Fi operation can lead to heating issues if the ESP32 is in a high-power use scenario for a prolonged period. Ensure proper ventilation if necessary.

Project: Static IP Configuration and Power Management

Object

To configure the ESP32 with a static IP address and custom hostname, and experiment with power management by adjusting Wi-Fi sleep settings.

Requirement

- ESP32 development board
- USB cable
- Arduino IDE

Circuit Connection

- **Serial Monitor**: Connect the ESP32 to your computer using a USB cable. This provides both power and allows you to view results on the serial monitor.

Circuit Analysis

- The ESP32 will connect to a Wi-Fi network with a static IP address and a custom hostname, ensuring easy identification on the network.
- Power management will be handled by toggling the Wi-Fi sleep mode, allowing you to observe the impact on the connection behavior and power consumption.

How to Work

1. Use *WiFi.config(ip, gateway, subnet)* to assign a static IP to the ESP32.
2. Set a custom hostname using *WiFi.setHostname(name)*.
3. Use *WiFi.setSleep(false)* to disable Wi-Fi sleep mode for continuous connectivity.
4. Display the connection status, IP address, and hostname on the serial monitor.

Use Syntax

```
WiFi.config(local_IP, gateway, subnet);
WiFi.setHostname("YourHostname");
WiFi.setSleep(false);
WiFi.begin(ssid, password);
```

Code

```
#include <WiFi.h>
const char ssid = "YourNetworkName";*
const char password = "YourPassword";*
IPAddress local_IP(192, 168, 1, 184);
IPAddress gateway(192, 168, 1, 1);
IPAddress subnet(255, 255, 255, 0);
void setup() {
  Serial.begin(115200);
  if (!WiFi.config(local_IP, gateway, subnet)) {
    Serial.println("Static IP Configuration Failed");
  } else {
    Serial.println("Static IP Configuration Successful");
  }
  WiFi.setHostname("ESP32_CustomHostname");
  WiFi.setSleep(false);
  WiFi.begin(ssid, password);
  Serial.println("Connecting to Wi-Fi...");
  while (WiFi.status() != WL_CONNECTED) {
    delay(1000);
    Serial.print(".");
  }
  Serial.println();
  Serial.println("Connected to Wi-Fi!");
  Serial.print("Hostname: ");
  Serial.println(WiFi.getHostname());
  Serial.print("IP Address: ");
  Serial.println(WiFi.localIP());
}
void loop() {
  // Your main code here
}
```

Code Walkthrough

- *#include <WiFi.h>*: Includes the library for Wi-Fi functions.
- *const char* ssid = "YourNetworkName"; const char* password = "YourPassword";*: Stores the Wi-Fi credentials.
- *IPAddress local_IP(192, 168, 1, 184); IPAddress gateway(192, 168, 1, 1); IPAddress subnet(255, 255, 255, 0);*: Configures the static IP, gateway, and subnet mask.
- *WiFi.config(local_IP, gateway, subnet);*: Assigns a static IP address to the ESP32.
- *WiFi.setHostname("ESP32_CustomHostname");*: Sets a custom hostname for easy identification on the network.
- *WiFi.setSleep(false);*: Disables sleep mode for continuous Wi-Fi connectivity.
- *WiFi.begin(ssid, password);*: Starts the connection to the specified Wi-Fi network.
- The connection status, IP address, and hostname are displayed on the serial monitor for verification.

Note

- Replace *"YourNetworkName"* and *"YourPassword"* with your Wi-Fi network credentials.
- A static IP ensures that the ESP32 always has the same address on the network, which simplifies remote access.
- Disabling sleep mode will increase power consumption. Use this option if uninterrupted network connectivity is required.
- You can experiment by toggling sleep mode on and off to observe differences in power usage and network stability.

Chapter-10 Web Server

1. Server Control Functions

begin() and handleClient()

begin() and *handleClient()* are functions used in Arduino programming to manage a web server on ESP32 or ESP8266 microcontrollers. *begin()* starts the web server, while *handleClient()* processes incoming client requests.

Why is Important?
These functions are important because they form the backbone of running a web server on ESP32 or ESP8266. *begin()* initializes the server to start listening for requests, and *handleClient()* must be called continuously to manage and respond to client requests, making it possible for users to interact with the ESP32 via a web page.

Syntax

```
server.begin();
server.handleClient();
```

Syntax Explanation

- *server:* Refers to the instance of the web server object, often declared using *WebServer server(port);*.
- *begin()*: Initializes the server, allowing it to start listening for client requests.
- *handleClient()*: Processes any incoming client requests. This function is typically called repeatedly within the *loop()* function to ensure all requests are handled.

Code Example

```
#include <WiFi.h> #include <WebServer.h>
const char ssid = "YourNetworkName";*
const char password = "YourPassword";*
WebServer server(80);
void handleRoot() {    server.send(200, "text/plain", "Hello, world!");
}
void setup() {    Serial.begin(115200);
  WiFi.begin(ssid, password);
  while (WiFi.status() != WL_CONNECTED) {    delay(1000);
Serial.print(".");    }
  Serial.println("Connected to Wi-Fi!");
  server.on("/", handleRoot);
  server.begin();
  Serial.println("Server started."); }
void loop() {    server.handleClient(); }
```

Notes

- *begin()* must be called after setting up the routes with *server.on()*.
- *handleClient()* should be called repeatedly, typically in the *loop()* function, to ensure the server handles all incoming requests in real-time.

Warnings

- Not calling *handleClient()* continuously will prevent the server from responding to client requests, causing the web interface to be unresponsive.
- Make sure that *begin()* is only called once to avoid restarting the server unnecessarily, which can disrupt the network connection.

Project: Basic Web Server

Object

To set up a basic web server on ESP32 that listens for incoming HTTP requests and serves a simple webpage.

Requirement

- ESP32 development board
- USB cable
- Arduino IDE

Circuit Connection

- **Serial Monitor**: Connect the ESP32 to your computer using a USB cable for power and serial communication. There are no additional hardware connections required for this project.

Circuit Analysis

- The ESP32 will use the Wi-Fi network to serve a web page.
- Once connected, any device on the same network can access the ESP32's IP address to view the hosted web page.

How to Work

1. Connect the ESP32 to your computer via USB and upload the code.
2. The ESP32 will connect to the specified Wi-Fi network and start the web server.
3. When a device on the same network sends an HTTP request to the ESP32's IP address, the server will respond with a message.
4. You can access the web page from any web browser by entering the ESP32's IP address.

Use Syntax

```
server.begin();
server.handleClient();
```

Code

```
#include <WiFi.h> #include <WebServer.h>
const char ssid = "YourNetworkName";*
const char password = "YourPassword";*
WebServer server(80);
void handleRoot() {
  server.send(200, "text/plain", "Hello, world!");
}
void setup() {
  Serial.begin(115200);
  WiFi.begin(ssid, password);
  while (WiFi.status() != WL_CONNECTED) {
    delay(1000);
    Serial.print(".");
  }
  Serial.println("Connected to Wi-Fi!");
  server.on("/", handleRoot);
  server.begin();
  Serial.println("Server started.");
}
void loop() {
  server.handleClient();
}
```

Code Walkthrough

- *#include <WiFi.h>, #include <WebServer.h>*: Includes the necessary libraries for handling Wi-Fi and web server functionality.
- *const char ssid = "YourNetworkName"; const char* password = "YourPassword";**: Stores the Wi-Fi network credentials.
- *WebServer server(80);*: Initializes the web server on port 80 (HTTP default port).
- *void handleRoot()*: Defines the function to handle requests to the root ("/") URL. Sends a "Hello, world!" response.

- *server.on("/", handleRoot);*: Registers the root URL ("/") with the *handleRoot()* function.
- *server.begin();*: Starts the web server, allowing it to listen for incoming requests.
- *server.handleClient();*: Called repeatedly in the *loop()* function to process and respond to incoming client requests.

Note

- Replace *"YourNetworkName"* and *"YourPassword"* with your actual Wi-Fi network credentials.
- The IP address of the ESP32 will be printed to the Serial Monitor after it connects to Wi-Fi. Use this IP address in a browser to access the server.
- Make sure your ESP32 and client device are connected to the same network to access the web server successfully.

2. Request Handling Functions

on() and onNotFound()

on() and *onNotFound()* are functions used in Arduino programming for ESP32 or ESP8266 to define how the web server should respond to specific HTTP requests. *on()* is used to register a URL path and specify a handler function for that path, while *onNotFound()* is used to handle requests that do not match any registered paths (404 errors).

Why is Important?
These functions are crucial for customizing the behavior of the web server by determining how it should respond to different requests. *on()* allows you to define multiple endpoints, such as "/on" or "/off" for controlling a device. *onNotFound()* helps provide a user-friendly response when a user requests a non-existent URL, enhancing the user experience.

Syntax

```
server.on("/path", HTTP_GET, handleFunction);
server.onNotFound(handleNotFound);
```

Syntax Explanation

- *server*: Refers to the instance of the web server object.
- *on("/path", HTTP_GET, handleFunction)*: Registers a route for a specific URL path ("/path") and a handler function (*handleFunction*) that executes when a client makes an HTTP GET request to that URL.
- *onNotFound(handleNotFound)*: Registers a handler function (*handleNotFound*) that is called when a client requests a URL that is not defined in the server.

Code Example

```
#include <WiFi.h> #include <WebServer.h>
const char ssid = "YourNetworkName";*
const char password = "YourPassword";*
WebServer server(80);
void handleRoot() {
  server.send(200, "text/plain", "Hello, world!");
}
void handleNotFound() {
  server.send(404, "text/plain", "404: Not Found");
}
void setup() {
  Serial.begin(115200);
  WiFi.begin(ssid, password);
  while (WiFi.status() != WL_CONNECTED) {
    delay(1000);
    Serial.print(".");
  }
  Serial.println("Connected to Wi-Fi!");
  server.on("/", HTTP_GET, handleRoot);
  server.onNotFound(handleNotFound);
  server.begin();
  Serial.println("Server started.");
}
void loop() {
  server.handleClient();
}
```

Notes

- *server.on()* must be called for each route you want to define. You can set up multiple routes for different purposes (e.g., "/on", "/off").
- *onNotFound()* is useful for handling all undefined routes with a custom response, such as displaying an error page or a custom message.

Warnings

- If *server.on()* is not called for a specific path, and *onNotFound()* is not defined, requests to undefined URLs may result in no response, leading to a poor user experience.
- Make sure the handler functions (like *handleRoot()*, *handleNotFound()*) are defined before using them in *server.on()* or *server.onNotFound()*.

Project: LED Control via Web Interface

Object
To control an LED connected to the ESP32 using a web page with HTML buttons.

Requirement

- ESP32 development board
- USB cable
- LED
- 220 ohm resistor
- Breadboard and jumper wires

Circuit Connection

- Connect the anode (longer leg) of the LED to GPIO pin 5 of the ESP32.
- Connect a 220 ohm resistor between the cathode (shorter leg) of the LED and the GND pin of the ESP32.

Circuit Analysis

- The ESP32 will serve a web page that has HTML buttons to control the state of the LED.
- The GPIO pin 5 will be set to HIGH or LOW based on the button clicked, thus turning the LED on or off.

How to Work

1. Set up the hardware by connecting the LED to GPIO pin 5 with a 220 ohm resistor.
2. Write the code to create a web server with two routes: "/on" to turn on the LED and "/off" to turn it off.
3. Access the ESP32's IP address from a web browser and use the buttons to control the LED.

Use Syntax

```
server.on("/on", HTTP_GET, handleLEDOn);
server.on("/off", HTTP_GET, handleLEDOff);
server.onNotFound(handleNotFound);
server.begin();
server.handleClient();
```

Code

```
#include <WiFi.h> #include <WebServer.h>
const char ssid = "YourNetworkName";*
const char password = "YourPassword";*
WebServer server(80);
const int ledPin = 5;
void handleLEDOn() {
  digitalWrite(ledPin, HIGH);
  server.send(200, "text/plain", "LED is ON");
}
void handleLEDOff() {
  digitalWrite(ledPin, LOW);
  server.send(200, "text/plain", "LED is OFF");
}
void handleNotFound() {
  server.send(404, "text/plain", "404: Not Found");
}
void setup() {
  Serial.begin(115200);
  pinMode(ledPin, OUTPUT);
  WiFi.begin(ssid, password);
  while (WiFi.status() != WL_CONNECTED) {
    delay(1000);
    Serial.print(".");
  }
  Serial.println("Connected to Wi-Fi!");
  server.on("/", HTTP_GET, {
    server.send(200, "text/html", "<h1>LED Control</h1><button
onclick="window.location.href='/on'">Turn On</button><button
onclick="window.location.href='/off'">Turn Off</button>");
  });
  server.on("/on", HTTP_GET, handleLEDOn);
  server.on("/off", HTTP_GET, handleLEDOff);
  server.onNotFound(handleNotFound);
  server.begin();
  Serial.println("Server started.");
}
void loop() {
  server.handleClient();
}
```

Code Walkthrough

- *#include <WiFi.h>*, *#include <WebServer.h>*: Include
  necessary libraries for Wi-Fi and web server functions.
- *const char* ssid = "YourNetworkName"; const char* password
  = "YourPassword";*: Store Wi-Fi network credentials.

- *const int ledPin = 5;*: Define the GPIO pin used for controlling the LED.
- *void handleLEDOn()* and *void handleLEDOff()*: Define functions to handle requests to turn the LED on or off.
- *server.on("/", HTTP_GET, { ... });*: Set up the root page with buttons to control the LED.
- *server.on("/on", HTTP_GET, handleLEDOn)* and *server.on("/off", HTTP_GET, handleLEDOff)*: Register the "/on" and "/off" routes and associate them with their respective handler functions.
- *server.onNotFound(handleNotFound)*: Handle 404 errors with a custom message.
- *server.begin()*: Start the web server.
- *server.handleClient()*: Continuously handle incoming requests.

Note

- Replace *"YourNetworkName"* and *"YourPassword"* with the actual Wi-Fi network credentials.
- Open the Serial Monitor to find the IP address of the ESP32. Enter the IP address in a browser to access the web page.
- The buttons on the webpage can be used to turn the LED on or off. Ensure the ESP32 and the browser are on the same Wi-Fi network for this to work properly.

3. Response Functions

Function: send(), sendHeader(), send_P()

send(), *sendHeader()*, and *send_P()* are functions used in Arduino programming for ESP32 or ESP8266 to send HTTP responses to clients. *send()* sends the entire response, *sendHeader()* is used to add custom HTTP headers, and *send_P()* is used to send content stored in program memory, which is helpful for saving RAM.

Why is Important?

These functions are important for creating dynamic web pages served by the ESP32 or ESP8266. *send()* allows you to provide the content of the response, while *sendHeader()* customizes the headers, which can be useful for setting content type or caching. *send_P()* helps in optimizing memory usage by storing large HTML or text files in program memory instead of dynamic memory.

Syntax

```
server.send(status_code, content_type, content);
server.sendHeader(header_name, header_value);
server.send_P(status_code, content_type, content);
```

Syntax Explanation

- *server*: Refers to the instance of the web server object.
- *send(status_code, content_type, content)*: Sends a complete HTTP response with the given status code (e.g., 200 for success), content type (e.g., "text/html"), and the content to be displayed.
- *sendHeader(header_name, header_value)*: Adds a specific header to the HTTP response, such as setting a cache-control header.
- *send_P(status_code, content_type, content)*: Sends content stored in program memory to save RAM. This is especially useful for large, static HTML content.

Code Example

```
#include <WiFi.h> #include <WebServer.h>
const char ssid = "YourNetworkName";*
const char password = "YourPassword";*
WebServer server(80);
const char htmlContent[] PROGMEM = "<html><body><h1>Hello from
ESP32!</h1></body></html>";
void handleRoot() {
  server.send(200, "text/html", "<h1>Welcome to the ESP32 Web
Server</h1>");
}
void handleCustomHeader() {
  server.sendHeader("Cache-Control", "no-cache");
```

```
    server.send(200, "text/plain", "This page should not be cached.");
}
void handleProgMem() {
    server.send_P(200, "text/html", htmlContent);
}
void setup() {
    Serial.begin(115200);
    WiFi.begin(ssid, password);
    while (WiFi.status() != WL_CONNECTED) {
        delay(1000);
        Serial.print(".");
    }
    Serial.println("Connected to Wi-Fi!");
    server.on("/", handleRoot);
    server.on("/nocache", handleCustomHeader);
    server.on("/progmem", handleProgMem);
    server.begin();
    Serial.println("Server started.");
}
void loop() {
    server.handleClient();
}
```

Notes

- *sendHeader()* must be called before *send()* to include the header in the response.
- Using *send_P()* helps conserve dynamic memory (RAM), which is particularly helpful on memory-constrained devices like ESP8266.

Warnings

- Make sure to use the correct content type to avoid rendering issues in the browser. For example, use *"text/html"* for HTML content and *"text/plain"* for plain text.
- Overuse of dynamic memory (*send()*) for large content might cause memory overflow issues, especially on the ESP8266 with limited RAM. Consider using *send_P()* to avoid such problems.

Project: "Temperature Monitoring Web Page"

The goal of this project is to display live temperature sensor readings on a web page hosted by the ESP32. The ESP32 will gather temperature data from a sensor and serve this data via a web page accessible through a local network.

Object:

The objective is to create a simple web page using the ESP32 that shows real-time temperature data gathered from a sensor.

Requirement:

- **ESP32** or **ESP8266** microcontroller
- **Temperature sensor** (e.g., DHT11, DHT22, or LM35)
- **Jumper wires**
- **Breadboard**
- **Arduino IDE** with the necessary libraries installed (WiFi, DHT, WebServer)

Circuit Connection:

1. **VCC Pin** (temperature sensor) -> **3.3V Pin** (ESP32)
2. **GND Pin** (temperature sensor) -> **GND Pin** (ESP32)
3. **Data Pin** (temperature sensor) -> **GPIO 4** (ESP32) (or another digital pin)

Circuit Analysis:

The temperature sensor measures the surrounding temperature and sends the data to the ESP32 via the data pin. The ESP32 processes this information and sends it to a client (a web browser) through a local network. The web server running on the ESP32 will handle HTTP requests from the browser, delivering the temperature data in a readable format.

How to work:

1. **ESP32 connects to Wi-Fi**: It connects to a local Wi-Fi network using the provided SSID and password.
2. **Temperature sensor collects data**: The sensor sends temperature readings to the ESP32.
3. **ESP32 hosts a web page**: The ESP32 acts as a web server and displays the temperature on a simple HTML web page when accessed from a browser.
4. **Live updates**: The web page can be refreshed to show new data as the temperature changes.

Use syntax:

```
server.on("/", HTTP_GET, handleRoot);
server.send(200, "text/html", webpage);
dht.readTemperature();
```

Code:

```
#include <WiFi.h> #include <WebServer.h> #include <DHT.h>
const char ssid = "your_SSID";*
const char password = "your_PASSWORD";*
WebServer server(80);
DHT dht(4, DHT11); // GPIO 4 for the sensor data pin
void setup() {
  Serial.begin(115200); // Start serial communication
  WiFi.begin(ssid, password); // Connect to Wi-Fi network
  while (WiFi.status() != WL_CONNECTED) {
    delay(1000);
    Serial.println("Connecting to WiFi...");
  }
  Serial.println("Connected to WiFi");
  dht.begin(); // Start the temperature sensor
  server.on("/", handleRoot); // Set up the web page
  server.begin();
  Serial.println("HTTP server started");
}
void loop() {
  server.handleClient(); // Handle any client requests
}
void handleRoot() {
  float temperature = dht.readTemperature(); // Read temperature from
the sensor
  String webpage = "<h1>Temperature Monitoring</h1>";
  webpage += "<p>Current Temperature: " + String(temperature) + "
°C</p>"; // Create the HTML content
  server.send(200, "text/html", webpage); // Send the HTML page to the
browser
}
```

Code Walkthrough:

- **Wi-Fi Setup**:
  WiFi.begin(ssid, password); connects the ESP32 to the Wi-Fi network using the provided SSID and password.

- **DHT Sensor Setup**:
  dht.begin(); initializes the DHT temperature sensor.
- **Web Server Setup**:
  server.on("/", handleRoot); registers the function
  handleRoot() to be called when a browser accesses the
  ESP32.
- **Temperature Reading**:
  float temperature = dht.readTemperature(); reads the
  temperature value from the sensor.
- **Serving the Web Page**:
  server.send(200, "text/html", webpage); sends the HTML
  content as a response to the client, which displays the
  temperature.

Note:

- Replace *your_SSID* and *your_PASSWORD* with the actual
  name and password of your Wi-Fi network.
- The web page is accessible by entering the ESP32's local IP
  address in a web browser after it connects to the Wi-Fi. The
  IP address can be found in the Serial Monitor.

4. Request Data Retrieval Functions

arg()

The **arg()** function is used to retrieve the value of a specific
argument passed in the URL of an HTTP request. It allows the
ESP32/ESP8266 web server to access client-provided data, such as
parameters in a form or URL query string.

Why is Important?
It is essential for handling dynamic input from the client, allowing you
to process data sent via GET or POST requests. This enables
interaction with the web server, such as controlling outputs or
adjusting settings based on client inputs.

Syntax

```
server.arg(name)
```

Syntax Explanation

- *name*: The name of the argument (parameter) to retrieve from the URL or form submission.

Code Example

```
String value = server.arg("temperature");
```

Notes

- This function is often used when handling forms or query parameters in the URL.

Warnings

- Ensure that the argument name is spelled correctly and exists in the URL. Otherwise, it will return an empty string.

---

uri()

The **uri()** function retrieves the Uniform Resource Identifier (URI) of the current HTTP request. This helps identify the path the client is requesting, enabling routing to the correct handler.

Why is Important?
It is critical for managing different routes in a web server, allowing the ESP32/ESP8266 to know which webpage or resource the client is asking for and execute the appropriate code.

Syntax

```
server.uri()
```

Syntax Explanation

- This function does not take any arguments and returns a string with the current URI.

Code Example

```
String requestedPage = server.uri();
```

Notes

- Use this function in routing scenarios where different actions are needed for different URIs.

Warnings

- The returned URI string is case-sensitive.

---

method()

The **method()** function is used to determine whether the incoming HTTP request is a GET or POST request. It allows the server to differentiate between read (GET) and write (POST) operations.

Why is Important?
This function is crucial for handling different types of requests correctly. GET is typically used for retrieving data, while POST is used for submitting data, and you must handle them differently on the server side.

Syntax

```
server.method()
```

Syntax Explanation

- It returns an integer indicating the HTTP method: *HTTP_GET* or *HTTP_POST*.

Code Example

```
if (server.method() == HTTP_POST) {
  // Handle POST request
}
```

Notes

- Commonly used to determine how to process incoming requests based on their method type.

Warnings

- Ensure you handle each method type properly to avoid unexpected server behavior.

---

hasArg()

The **hasArg()** function checks if a specific argument is present in the HTTP request. It allows the web server to confirm whether the client has sent a particular parameter.

Why is Important?

This function is vital for ensuring required parameters are included in requests, improving error handling and preventing missing data from causing server issues.

Syntax

```
server.hasArg(name)
```

Syntax Explanation

- *name*: The name of the argument to check.

Code Example

```
if (server.hasArg("temperature")) {
  // Argument exists
}
```

Notes

- Use this to ensure critical arguments are present before processing a request.

Warnings

- If the argument does not exist, it will return *false*. Handle this case to avoid errors in processing.

Project: "Wi-Fi Network Configurator"

The goal of this project is to allow users to configure Wi-Fi settings on an ESP32 device through a simple web form hosted by the ESP32. Users can connect to the ESP32's network, enter the Wi-Fi credentials, and the ESP32 will use these credentials to connect to the specified network.

Object:

To create a web-based interface hosted by the ESP32 where users can select and configure Wi-Fi settings (SSID and password) via a web form.

Requirement:

- **ESP32** or **ESP8266** microcontroller
- **Breadboard**
- **Jumper wires**
- **Arduino IDE** with the necessary libraries installed (WiFi, WebServer, etc.)

Circuit Connection:

The ESP32 will be directly connected to your computer via USB for programming. No external hardware is necessary for this project unless you want to include status indicators like LEDs.

Circuit Analysis:

This project involves only the ESP32, which will act as a Wi-Fi access point (AP) and web server. The ESP32 will start in AP mode, allowing a user to connect to it and enter Wi-Fi credentials using a web form. After submission, the ESP32 will use the provided details to connect to the chosen network.

How to work:

1. **ESP32 creates a Wi-Fi Access Point (AP)**:
   The ESP32 starts as an access point, allowing nearby devices to connect to it directly.
2. **User connects to the ESP32's network**:
   Using a smartphone or computer, the user connects to the ESP32's Wi-Fi network.
3. **User accesses the web page**:
   The user opens a web page (e.g., *192.168.4.1*) where the form for entering Wi-Fi credentials is displayed.
4. **User submits Wi-Fi credentials**:
   The user enters the Wi-Fi SSID and password, which the ESP32 processes.
5. **ESP32 connects to the selected Wi-Fi network**:
   The ESP32 then disconnects from AP mode and connects to the provided Wi-Fi network.

Use syntax:

```
WiFi.softAP(ssid, password);
server.arg("ssid");
server.arg("password");
WiFi.begin(ssid, password);
```

Code:

```
#include <WiFi.h> #include <WebServer.h>
WebServer server(80);
const char ap_ssid = "ESP32_Config";*
const char ap_password = "password";*
void setup() {
  Serial.begin(115200);
  WiFi.softAP(ap_ssid, ap_password); // Create Access Point
  Serial.println("Access Point Created");
  server.on("/", handleRoot); // Serve form on the root
  server.on("/submit", handleForm); // Handle form submission
  server.begin();
```

```
  Serial.println("Server started");
}
void loop() {
  server.handleClient(); // Handle client requests
}
void handleRoot() {
  String webpage = "Wi-Fi Configuration";
  webpage += "<form action='/submit' method='POST'>";
  webpage += "SSID: <input type='text' name='ssid'><br>";
  webpage += "Password: <input type='text' name='password'><br>";
  webpage += "<input type='submit' value='Submit'></form>";
  server.send(200, "text/html", webpage);
}
void handleForm() {
  String ssid = server.arg("ssid"); // Get SSID
  String password = server.arg("password"); // Get password
  Serial.println("Connecting to WiFi...");
  WiFi.begin(ssid.c_str(), password.c_str()); // Connect to the Wi-Fi
  server.send(200, "text/html", "Connecting to Wi-Fi...");
}
```

Code Walkthrough:

1. **Wi-Fi Access Point Setup**:
   o *WiFi.softAP(ap_ssid, ap_password);* creates an
     access point named "ESP32_Config" with the
     password "password".
2. **Handling Web Page Requests**:
   o *server.on("/", handleRoot);* serves a web form to the
     client when the ESP32 receives a request at the root
     URL ("/").
   o *server.on("/submit", handleForm);* handles form
     submissions when the user enters the Wi-Fi
     credentials.
3. **Form Submission Handling**:
   o *server.arg("ssid");* and *server.arg("password");*
     retrieve the SSID and password entered by the user.
   o *WiFi.begin(ssid.c_str(), password.c_str());* instructs
     the ESP32 to connect to the Wi-Fi network using the
     provided credentials.

Note:

- Replace *ap_ssid* and *ap_password* with your preferred network name and password for the access point.
- After the user submits the form, the ESP32 will try to connect to the specified Wi-Fi network using the provided SSID and password.

arg()

The **arg()** function retrieves the value of a specific argument passed in an HTTP request URL or POST data. It allows the ESP32/ESP8266 to access data sent by a client, such as values from forms or query parameters.

Why is Important?
This function is crucial for handling user inputs in web forms or URLs. It enables the server to process data sent by the client, such as form fields, and react accordingly.

Syntax

```
server.arg(name)
```

Syntax Explanation

- *name*: The name of the argument (parameter) that you want to retrieve.

Code Example

```
String username = server.arg("username");
```

Notes

- This function is typically used to handle form data or URL query parameters.

Warnings

- If the specified argument does not exist, the function will return an empty string. Ensure that the argument name matches being sent by the client.

---

hasArg()

The **hasArg()** function checks whether a specific argument is present in an HTTP request. It is used to confirm whether the client has provided the necessary parameter before trying to retrieve its value.

Why is Important?
This function helps to prevent errors by verifying that required parameters are included in the request before accessing them. It's important for ensuring smooth data handling and avoiding missing or incomplete data submissions.

Syntax

```
server.hasArg(name)
```

Syntax Explanation
- *name*: The name of the argument (parameter) to check for.

Code Example

```
if (server.hasArg("username")) {
  String username = server.arg("username");
}
```

Notes

- Use this function to verify that the necessary arguments exist before trying to retrieve them.

Warnings

- If the argument is not present, it will return *false*. Be sure to handle cases where the argument is missing to avoid unexpected behavior.

Project: "IoT Control with Parameters"

The objective of this project is to control the brightness of an LED using a web interface hosted by the ESP32/ESP8266. A parameter is sent from the browser, allowing the user to adjust the brightness of the LED by changing its PWM (Pulse Width Modulation) value.

Object:

To create a simple web interface that allows users to control the brightness of an LED by sending a PWM value from a browser to the ESP32/ESP8266.

Requirement:

- **ESP32** or **ESP8266** microcontroller
- **LED** (any color)
- **1kΩ Resistor**
- **Jumper wires**
- **Breadboard**
- **Arduino IDE** with the necessary libraries installed (WiFi, WebServer)

Circuit Connection:

1. **LED Anode (long leg) -> PWM-capable GPIO pin** (e.g., GPIO 5 on ESP32)
2. **LED Cathode (short leg) -> Resistor (1kΩ) -> GND (ESP32)**

Circuit Analysis:

The circuit consists of a single LED connected to one of the ESP32/ESP8266's GPIO pins that supports PWM. By using PWM, we can control the brightness of the LED by adjusting the duty cycle of the PWM signal. The user will send a value between 0 (off) and 255 (full brightness) from the web interface to control the LED's brightness.

How to work:

1. **ESP32/ESP8266 creates a Wi-Fi Access Point (AP)**:
   The ESP32 will create its own Wi-Fi network or connect to an existing one.
2. **User connects to the ESP32's network**:
   Users can connect to the ESP32's network via a browser (e.g., typing the ESP32's IP address).
3. **User sends a PWM value**:
   The user enters a brightness value (0-255) in a web form or URL query parameter to adjust the brightness of the LED.
4. **ESP32/ESP8266 adjusts the LED brightness**:
   The ESP32 receives the value from the browser and adjusts the PWM signal, controlling the brightness of the LED accordingly.

Use syntax:

```
analogWrite(pin, value);
server.arg("brightness");
WiFi.begin(ssid, password);
```

Code:

```
#include <WiFi.h> #include <WebServer.h>
const char ssid = "your_SSID";*
const char password = "your_PASSWORD";*
WebServer server(80);
int ledPin = 5; // GPIO pin for LED
void setup() {
  Serial.begin(115200);
  WiFi.begin(ssid, password); // Connect to Wi-Fi
  while (WiFi.status() != WL_CONNECTED) {
    delay(1000);
    Serial.println("Connecting to WiFi...");
  }
  Serial.println("Connected to WiFi");
  server.on("/", handleRoot); // Serve main page
  server.on("/control", handleControl); // Handle brightness control
  server.begin();
```

```
  Serial.println("Server started");
  pinMode(ledPin, OUTPUT);
}
void loop() {
  server.handleClient(); // Handle client requests
}
void handleRoot() {
  String webpage = "Control LED Brightness";
  webpage += "<form action='/control' method='GET'>";
  webpage += "Brightness (0-255): <input type='number'
name='brightness'><br>";
  webpage += "<input type='submit' value='Set Brightness'></form>";
  server.send(200, "text/html", webpage);
}
void handleControl() {
  if (server.hasArg("brightness")) {
    int brightness = server.arg("brightness").toInt(); // Get
brightness value
    analogWrite(ledPin, brightness); // Set LED brightness
    String message = "LED brightness set to: " + String(brightness);
    server.send(200, "text/html", message);
  } else {
    server.send(200, "text/html", "No brightness value received");
  }
}
```

Code Walkthrough:

1. **Wi-Fi Setup**
   o *WiFi.begin(ssid, password);* connects the ESP32 to
      the specified Wi-Fi network.
2. **Web Server Setup**
   o *server.on("/", handleRoot);* defines the root route ("/")
      to serve a basic form that allows users to input a
      brightness value.
   o *server.on("/control", handleControl);* handles the URL
      route "/control" where the brightness value is sent
      from the form.
3. **Brightness Control**
   o *server.arg("brightness");* retrieves the PWM
      brightness value from the form.
   o *analogWrite(ledPin, brightness);* adjusts the
      brightness of the LED using PWM.
4. **Handling Form Submission**

- If the user submits a valid brightness value, the ESP32 adjusts the LED's brightness and sends a confirmation message back to the browser.

Note:

- Replace *your_SSID* and *your_PASSWORD* with the actual Wi-Fi credentials.
- Adjust the GPIO pin according to your ESP32 or ESP8266 setup.
- Ensure the browser sends valid brightness values (0-255).

Chapter-11 ESP Deep Sleep Mode

What is Deep Sleep?

Deep Sleep is a special low-power mode used by devices like the ESP32 microcontroller to conserve energy. Think of it like putting your device into a "power nap" where most of its systems shut down, except for a tiny part called the **Ultra Low Power (ULP) coprocessor**. This ULP coprocessor acts like a minimal monitoring system, keeping an eye on things while the rest of the device is essentially asleep.

Why Is Deep Sleep Important?

Deep Sleep is crucial for reducing power consumption. This is especially beneficial for **battery-powered devices**, where conserving energy is essential to extend the battery life. For example, if you're using an ESP32 for a smart sensor that doesn't need to be awake all the time (like checking the temperature a few times an hour), Deep Sleep allows the device to run **longer without needing frequent recharges**. Essentially, it allows the device to save energy by sleeping most of the time, only waking up when it needs to perform specific tasks.

How Does It Work?

When the ESP32 enters Deep Sleep:

- **Most components power down**: The main processor, Wi-Fi, and Bluetooth are turned off.
- **ULP coprocessor remains active**: This coprocessor can perform very basic tasks like reading sensors and deciding if it needs to wake up the main system.
- The ESP32 wakes up when specific triggers happen, like a timer or an external event, allowing it to perform its tasks before going back to sleep.

Why Should You Use Deep Sleep?

Using Deep Sleep is especially recommended in scenarios where:

- You have **limited power availability**, such as battery-operated gadgets like remote sensors or wearables.
- You need to design an **energy-efficient system** that can function independently for weeks or months without frequent user interaction.

In summary, Deep Sleep is a practical way for devices like the ESP32 to save energy by reducing power usage when full processing power is not needed.

2. Entering Deep Sleep

Function to Enter Deep Sleep

Deep Sleep mode in the ESP32 is a power-saving state where most of the device's functions are shut down. The function *esp_deep_sleep_start()* is used to enter this mode, allowing the ESP32 to save energy until a defined wake-up source triggers it to become active again.

Why is Important
Using *esp_deep_sleep_start()* is important for battery-powered

applications because it helps to significantly extend battery life. By turning off most of the ESP32's features when they aren't needed, you can achieve a much lower power consumption, which is ideal for devices that need to operate for extended periods without recharging.

Syntax

```
esp_deep_sleep_start();
```

Syntax Explanation

esp_deep_sleep_start() initiates the deep sleep mode for the ESP32. Once this function is called, the ESP32 will power down its main components and only resume operation when an appropriate wake-up source is triggered.

Code Example

```
esp_sleep_enable_timer_wakeup(10 * 1000000);
esp_deep_sleep_start();
```

Notes

- Make sure to configure a wake-up source (like a timer or an external pin) before calling *esp_deep_sleep_start()*, or the ESP32 will remain in deep sleep indefinitely.
- The wake-up time configuration should be done using functions like *esp_sleep_enable_timer_wakeup()*.

Warnings

- When in deep sleep, data stored in RAM will be lost. Ensure that any important information is stored in a persistent way, such as in non-volatile memory.

- After waking up, the ESP32 resets itself, meaning that the code will start running from the beginning, similar to a fresh power-up.

Set Deep Sleep Duration

esp_deep_sleep(duration_in_us) is used to put the ESP32 into deep sleep mode for a specified amount of time. The duration is specified in microseconds, and after this duration has elapsed, the ESP32 will automatically wake up.

Why is Important
Using *esp_deep_sleep(duration_in_us)* is important when you need the ESP32 to enter a low-power state for a specific period. This is particularly useful for tasks where the device only needs to be active at set intervals, like reading sensor data once every few minutes. By setting a specific sleep duration, you can further optimize power usage, extending the battery life of your device.

Syntax

```
esp_deep_sleep(duration_in_us);
```

Syntax Explanation
esp_deep_sleep(duration_in_us) initiates deep sleep for the ESP32, where *duration_in_us* represents the length of time (in microseconds) that the device will remain in deep sleep before waking up.

Code Example

```
esp_deep_sleep(5000000); // Enter deep sleep for 5 seconds
```

Notes

- Be sure to convert your required duration into microseconds (e.g., 5 seconds equals 5,000,000 microseconds).
- This function will reset the ESP32 after the specified time, meaning it will start the program from the beginning upon wake-up.

Warnings

- Data stored in RAM is lost during deep sleep, so make sure to save any important data in non-volatile storage.
- The timer accuracy can be influenced by factors such as temperature or supply voltage, so it's important to keep that in mind for time-sensitive applications.

Project: "Periodic Sensor Reading"

To create a project that wakes up the ESP32 every 30 minutes to simulate a task, then enters deep sleep again to save power.

Requirement:

- ESP32 microcontroller
- Power supply (battery)

Circuit Connection:

- Connect the ESP32 to a stable power source.

Circuit Analysis:
In this simple setup, there are no external components. The ESP32 will operate independently, waking up every 30 minutes to simulate a task. This project demonstrates how to use deep sleep to extend battery life for periodic tasks.

How to work:

1. When powered on, the ESP32 will simulate performing a task by printing a message to the serial monitor.

2. After the task, the ESP32 will enter deep sleep for 30 minutes using *esp_deep_sleep(1800000000);*.
3. The ESP32 will automatically wake up after 30 minutes, simulate the task again, and repeat the process.

Code:

```
void setup() {
Serial.begin(115200);
Serial.println("ESP32 is awake and performing a task...");
esp_deep_sleep(1800000000); // Enter deep sleep for 30 minutes (30 * 60
* 1,000,000 microseconds)
}
void loop() {
// This code won't run as the ESP32 is in deep sleep mode
}
```

Code Walkthrough:

- *void setup()*: This function runs once when the ESP32 wakes up. It prints a message to indicate that it is awake and then calls the *esp_deep_sleep(1800000000);* function to put the ESP32 into deep sleep for 30 minutes.
- *esp_deep_sleep(1800000000);*: The function takes an argument in microseconds, setting the ESP32 to sleep for 30 minutes (30 * 60 * 1,000,000 microseconds).
- *void loop()*: The loop function is empty because the ESP32 enters deep sleep after executing the code in *setup()*, and it doesn't require continuous execution.

Note:

- Ensure that the power supply is stable while using deep sleep mode.
- Since data in RAM is lost during deep sleep, any critical information should be saved in non-volatile storage if needed.
- Upon waking up, the ESP32 restarts from the *setup()* function, behaving as if it was just powered on.

3. Wake-Up Sources

Timer Wake-Up

The ESP32 can be configured to wake up from deep sleep after a specific time interval using the function *esp_sleep_enable_timer_wakeup(duration_in_us)*. This feature is useful for scheduling the ESP32 to perform a task periodically without requiring external interaction.

Why is Important

Using *esp_sleep_enable_timer_wakeup(duration_in_us)* is crucial for applications where the ESP32 needs to conserve energy and wake up at regular intervals. This is especially helpful in battery-powered systems, allowing the ESP32 to sleep for most of the time and only wake up when needed, thus optimizing battery life.

Syntax

```
esp_sleep_enable_timer_wakeup(duration_in_us);
```

Syntax Explanation

esp_sleep_enable_timer_wakeup(duration_in_us) sets the duration for the ESP32 to remain in deep sleep before waking up. The parameter *duration_in_us* specifies the time interval in microseconds.

Code Example

```
esp_sleep_enable_timer_wakeup(60000000); // Set timer to wake up after
1 minute
esp_deep_sleep_start(); // Enter deep sleep mode
```

Notes

- Make sure to call *esp_sleep_enable_timer_wakeup(duration_in_us)* before *esp_deep_sleep_start()* to ensure the ESP32 knows when to wake up.
- The *duration_in_us* should be specified in microseconds (1 second = 1,000,000 microseconds).

Warnings

- If no wake-up source is specified, the ESP32 will stay in deep sleep indefinitely.
- Ensure that any important data is stored in non-volatile memory, as the ESP32 will reset upon waking up, similar to a power-on reset.

Touchpad Wake-Up

The ESP32 can wake up from deep sleep using its touch-sensitive GPIO pins. This feature allows the ESP32 to wake up when a user touches a specific pin, making it ideal for user interaction without additional hardware like buttons.

Why is Important

Touchpad wake-up is useful for applications where you want an interactive way to bring the ESP32 out of deep sleep. It's particularly handy in situations requiring a low-power setup, as it allows the user to wake up the device on demand without consuming much power, making it suitable for battery-powered devices and interactive projects.

Syntax

```
esp_sleep_enable_touchpad_wakeup();
```

Syntax Explanation

esp_sleep_enable_touchpad_wakeup() configures the ESP32 to wake up from deep sleep when one of the touch-sensitive pins is touched. This command must be used before entering deep sleep to set the wake-up source.

Code Example

```
touchAttachInterrupt(T0, callback, threshold_value);
esp_sleep_enable_touchpad_wakeup();
esp_deep_sleep_start();
```

Notes

- You need to configure the touchpad pin with *touchAttachInterrupt()* to set up which pin will act as a wake-up source.
- Different touchpad GPIOs are available on the ESP32, and each can be assigned for different user interactions.

Warnings

- Touch sensitivity may vary depending on environmental factors like humidity and temperature, which can affect how the ESP32 interprets a touch.
- False triggering can occur due to electrical noise, so it is important to calibrate the touch sensitivity appropriately.

External Wake-Up (GPIO)

External wake-up using *esp_sleep_enable_ext0_wakeup(pin, level)* allows the ESP32 to wake up from deep sleep mode when an external signal is detected on a specific GPIO pin. This is useful for applications requiring a hardware trigger, such as a button press or an external sensor.

Why is Important

External wake-up is important for scenarios where the ESP32 needs to respond to real-world events. For instance, a button press can trigger the ESP32 to wake up and perform a specific task. This helps in saving power by keeping the ESP32 in deep sleep mode until an event occurs, making it ideal for interactive, battery-powered devices.

Syntax

```
esp_sleep_enable_ext0_wakeup(pin, level);
```

Syntax Explanation

esp_sleep_enable_ext0_wakeup(pin, level) sets a specific GPIO pin (*pin*) as a wake-up source and specifies the signal level (*level*) to trigger the wake-up (0 for low level, 1 for high level).

Code Example

```
esp_sleep_enable_ext0_wakeup(GPIO_NUM_4, 0);
esp_deep_sleep_start();
```

Notes

- The pin specified must be RTC-enabled, as only specific GPIOs can be used for external wake-up.
- This method is often used for simple triggers like button presses, where a low or high signal indicates a wake-up event.

Warnings

- The signal level must remain stable until the ESP32 fully wakes up; otherwise, it might fail to wake up properly.

- Debouncing may be required when using mechanical switches, as bouncing signals could trigger multiple wake-ups unintentionally.

Project: "Touch-Activated Light"

To create a project where the ESP32 is put into deep sleep mode and wakes up when a specific touch-sensitive area is touched, simulating the activation of a light.

Requirement:

- ESP32 microcontroller
- LED (optional, to simulate the light activation)
- Resistor (220 ohms for LED)
- Jumper wires
- Breadboard

Circuit Connection:

- Connect an LED to GPIO 2 of the ESP32.
- Connect a resistor (220 ohms) in series with the LED to limit current.
- Connect the ground terminal of the LED to GND of the ESP32.

Circuit Analysis:

The ESP32 is configured to wake up when a touch-sensitive pin (e.g., T0) is touched. Upon wake-up, the ESP32 will turn on an LED, simulating the activation of a light. The use of deep sleep mode allows the system to save power, only activating when user interaction is detected.

How to work:

1. Initially, the ESP32 will be in deep sleep mode, conserving power.
2. When a user touches the specified touch-sensitive area (connected to T0), the ESP32 wakes up.
3. The ESP32 turns on the LED to simulate a light being activated.
4. After a short period, the ESP32 enters deep sleep again, waiting for the next interaction.

Code:

```
#define TOUCH_PIN T0 #define LED_PIN 2
void setup() {
pinMode(LED_PIN, OUTPUT);
Serial.begin(115200);
touchAttachInterrupt(TOUCH_PIN, callback, threshold_value);
esp_sleep_enable_touchpad_wakeup();
Serial.println("ESP32 is awake, turning on the LED...");
digitalWrite(LED_PIN, HIGH);
delay(5000); // Keep LED on for 5 seconds
digitalWrite(LED_PIN, LOW);
esp_deep_sleep_start();
}
void loop() {
// No code needed here, as ESP32 stays in deep sleep after setup
}
```

Code Walkthrough:

- *#define TOUCH_PIN T0*: Defines the touch pin that will wake up the ESP32 when touched.
- *#define LED_PIN 2*: Defines the pin connected to the LED.
- *touchAttachInterrupt(TOUCH_PIN, callback, threshold_value);*: Configures the touchpad pin to trigger an interrupt when touched.
- *esp_sleep_enable_touchpad_wakeup();*: Enables the wake-up feature for the specified touchpad pin.
- *digitalWrite(LED_PIN, HIGH);*: Turns on the LED to simulate light activation.
- *delay(5000);*: Keeps the LED on for 5 seconds before turning it off.
- *esp_deep_sleep_start();*: Puts the ESP32 back into deep sleep mode.

Note:

- Ensure to calibrate the touchpad sensitivity (*threshold_value*) for reliable wake-up.
- For energy-efficient operation, minimize the delay duration for which the LED stays on.